CAERPHILLY COUNTY BOROUGH

3 8030 08333 3396

Meeting your Dream Man

and Keeping Him

D1514205

Meeting your Dream Man
and Keeping Him

Robyn Partridge

First published in 2016 by New Holland Publishers Pty Ltd
London • Sydney • Auckland

The Chandlery Unit 704 50 Westminster Bridge Road
London SE1 7QY United Kingdom
1/66 Gibbes Street Chatswood NSW 2067 Australia
5/39 Woodside Ave Northcote, Auckland 0627 New Zealand

www.newhollandpublishers.com

Copyright © 2015 New Holland Publishers Pty Ltd
Copyright © 2015 in text: Robyn Partridge
Copyright © 2015 in images: Shutterstock

All rights reserved. No part of this publication may be
reproduced, stored in a retrieval system or transmitted, in any
form or by any means, electronic, mechanical, photocopying,
recording or otherwise, without the prior written permission
of the publishers and copyright holders.

A record of this book is held at the British Library and the
National Library of Australia.

ISBN 9781742578019

Managing Director: Fiona Schultz
Publisher: Alan Whiticker
Project Editor: Jessica McNamara
Cover design: Lorena Susak
Designer: Andrew Davies
Production Director: Olga Dementiev
Printer: Toppan Leefung Printing Limited
10 9 8 7 6 5 4 3 2 1

Keep up with New Holland Publishers on Facebook
www.facebook.com/NewHollandPublishers

I dedicate this book to my loving husband, best friend and partner in life.

Without your support and love I am only half a person. Thank you for being there when I need you – I know I can always count on you.

Foreword

When I first started to write this book, my main aim was to share my experiences with other women who were looking for the love of their lives. I thought my stance would be pro-female, but as I wrote, I discovered how old-fashioned my ideas really were. Am I not the modern woman that I thought I was? What is the meaning of 'modern'? Is it a new trend that won't last? Hmm, I don't know about that, but I have come to realize that my core beliefs about the relationships of men and women are indeed timeless – tested and proven by many.

In this book, you will read interviews with fabulous couples offering insight into their methods of maintaining loving and sustainable relationships and marriages that have stood the test of time – most of them are in the very respectable 25–40 year marks. Such relationships are not easy to achieve if couples are ill-equipped to deal with life's problems, big and small.

I would like you to read this book with the understanding that these words are my opinions only, based on my personal experiences in my own relationship. These ideas and words I have come to believe in are founded on what I've learned from a few relationship mistakes of my own as well.

I'm now enjoying a wonderful marriage to my own dream man. I don't promise my tips will work for all of you, but they are definitely worth trying!

If you feel that you have met your dream man already and would like to know how to *keep* him – just follow some of the ideas in this book. As you will see from the interview section, there are many other women out there who are married to their dream man and agree with the principles discussed.

Most of my advice for meeting a man whom you share similar interests with is focused on dating sites. This is where I had my best opportunities and met my husband. So, while online dating is certainly extensively covered in this book, there are plenty of other ways to meet your dream man, which I will tell you about so don't think you are limited to the method that worked for me.

My first assumption when writing this guide was that my readers would like to meet their dream man and continue through life having a long and happy relationship.

My second assumption was that they would be prepared *to put in the work* to fulfill those desires.

My third assumption was that the reader should be in

a mutually agreeable relationship to start with, if they are looking to *improve* their current relationship.

This book is not for anyone in a physically or emotionally abusive relationship. If you are in an abusive relationship you can seek help by visiting the International Directory of Domestic Violence Agencies online for a list of help lines and crisis centers.

I would also like to point out that some of my opinions won't cover every woman's situation, as my writing, after all, is based on my own personal experiences.

You may not agree with everything I have written, but even if you take a little bit, I hope you may use my tips to improve your relationship and put yourself on the path to many years of happiness. Use these suggestions for a few weeks and with a little perseverance and you may be surprised. Once you commence reading, you'll find it's not that easy and takes plenty of work, but in my mind it is all worth it and will be for you, too!

So there you have it ladies! Start reading and I wish you all the best of luck on your path to find love and happiness. I've included some pages for notes at the back of this book, so you can make notes and log your progress on any hints or tips that you may be trying out.

CHAPTER 1

Who are you and what do you want in life?

If you have just purchased this book, welcome! You are one of thousands of women on the serious journey to meet the man of their dreams.

Let me tell you right here in the first paragraph – do not be under any false illusions. This is hard work and your dream man will not present himself on your doorstep. You must treat this goal as a project and give it constant daily thought and attention if you wish to achieve your dream. If you feel you are up for this worthy challenge, please read on, because, speaking from personal experience, it is well worth the effort.

When I first started on my journey to find true love after my divorce I was very weary and didn't understand the possibilities that were open to me. I thought I was probably in a small group of people in their early 40s destined to be alone. Little did I know that there was a whole new world out there waiting for me, filled with divorced people just like me. I'd come out of my divorce feeling exhausted and with low self-esteem. When I realized that there were others my own age in the same situation, my spirits were lifted, and I realized there was the possibility of finding true love after all.

I hope by sharing my opinions, experiences and thoughts with you that you might gain some useful tips on how to go about finding your dream man.

Almost three decades ago, in the back of my diary I started a list of the 20 dream man qualities that I thought were important if I was to meet a man with whom I could share a future. One divorce and a couple of bad relationships later, I came across that old diary and the list. Even though by now it was torn and battered, I added another 20 qualities I wanted.

The importance of these qualities and personal traits became evident after my experiences with choosing the wrong relationship partners. Life and experience are great teachers, but some of us take a little longer than others to actually learn the lesson, so we have to redo the class no matter how many times it takes. This time, I was very specific with my additions to the list, and through experience realized there was so much more to a relationship than what I had on my original list.

It wasn't until after I married my darling husband about two years later that I turned to the back of this old diary and was able to give each item a big tick. This was a profound moment for me, realizing at that moment that I had never lost sight of what I wanted – and that it is possible to have everything you ask for if you put it down on paper and reach out to the universe.

If you are at the stage of wanting a life partner, it is extremely important to have a good understanding of who you are – good and bad. If you are not happy within yourself, you would be very wise to take some time out to do some counseling sessions until you feel comfortable with who you are. I'm a passionate advocate of counseling, and I think it does the world of good for everyone just to talk to an expert who may be able to put things in perspective for you or may be help you deal with the re-occurring errors in judgement you may be making.

My first piece of advice to you, therefore, is to sit down and make a very serious list of all the desirable qualities and personality traits you would desire in your partner.

Be specific – don't just write 'must be good looking'. This is far too much of a generalization. You must describe what that means to you. Your idea of good looks may be completely different to the next person's idea. Detail what 'good looking' means to you – short, tall, blonde, dark, fair, tanned, slim, muscular …. Some of the things I had on my list were: he must be kind, loves good food and wine, consid-erate, no more than five years older than myself, exercises regularly, sensible and practical – just to name a few.

My list had 40 items on it that were important to me. This is *your* list and so it is unique to you.

You are asking for what *you* want, not what everyone else thinks you should have.

Above all, do not get carried away with the physical. Once you have mind contact, the physical interest will follow naturally. Remember you are looking for a life partner not a male model! Creating this list is just the start and I'll be very clear about something else. This is not just about you. If you are fortunate to meet the man of your dreams, you had better be prepared to give him what he desires as well. Maybe he has his own list. A good relationship is hard work, and you should always give more than you take. So, now that we have an understanding of what we are about to undertake we should get started.

My quest to find my dream man after my divorce became my project. At that stage of my life I didn't believe in meeting someone by chance. I felt that I didn't have the luxury of time and wanted to be in a great relationship as soon as possible, so I put effort in each day to try and make contact with new people. The road I eventually went down was the electronic one, which I will describe in more detail in a later chapter. I was so fortunate to meet the person I was looking for, but there are many ways of meeting people.

As much as I would love to, I can't take each of you by the hand and introduce you to Mr Right. You have to be prepared to get out there and experience life to its fullest. Travel, networking, sports clubs, electronic dating – go anywhere that like-minded people get together and communicate. Just make all the right opportunities for yourself and ask lots of questions of your new acquaintances. Don't be nosey, but find out what their interests and likes/dislikes are. You may have similar interests that could lead to something.

Meeting the man of your dreams will enhance your life. I've always wished for a loving partner to share my life and be by my side.

I believe the most precious thing on earth for two people in a relationship is to have unconditional love for each other. A strong couple can achieve their goals easier than a single person. Depending on your goals this may not always be the case, but in general I think it has truth.

CHAPTER 2

Making your list

Okay, ladies, it's time to make your list of requirements and wishes for your dream partner. This is a very serious task and you must approach it seriously.

If you are having trouble starting your list, just begin making notes of what you *don't* want. This will give you the negative opposites of the positive things that you *do* want included in your next relationship. Think about your past relationships and the traits of your previous partner/s that you do not want to be repeated in future. Be careful not to include traits on your list that you have already experienced in previous relationships. If you are including too many of these, you may end up with what you have already experienced. Looking for something different is a good thing.

I had to change my views on what I was looking for in a relationship to actually achieve my goal of meeting the perfect partner. You may be surprised at how quickly your list grows once you start to write down all the negatives. These can be about yourself as well as previous partners. During this stage, you are taking a look back at yourself and the choices you made that may not have been the best.

Be very specific when making your list and choose your words carefully. The saying 'You might just get what you wish for' has proven true for myself many times. Start thinking about all the things in life that you enjoy participating in and make sure you include these things on your list that would be compatible with your partner.

There is no point noting down all of your ideal qualities in a man if you don't have similar traits yourself. Don't ask for someone who is kind and generous if you are not yourself. How can you ask for someone that looks after their body when you don't? If you do find you have listed some great characteristics that you don't have at present, then maybe you should entertain the idea of obtaining these yourself through changes in lifestyle or attitude. If you have asked for someone who is thoughtful and caring, you had better make sure that you have these qualities yourself. Remember, this is a two-sided relationship and not one where just you will be receiving care and thoughtfulness.

Handwritten lists are far more meaningful and personal than computer-printed lists, so that is why I say use pen and paper. If you decide to keep your list nearby, or in the back of a diary, each time you look at it you will recognize the handwriting and remember that these are your goals and how much they mean to you.

Concentrate on the core characteristics and traits that make up the person as a whole. Who this person is on the inside is far more crucial to the way you are treated than their external looks. Once you have thought carefully about the inner characteristics, you can make a list of the things that may attract you physically – such as someone who enjoys fitness and takes pride in their appearance. I have generally found that people that take pride in their homes and their appearance take pride in most other aspects of their lives, so these are very positive requirements you may like to include on your list. Life is too short to be unhappy.

Here are some of the things that could be on your list:

1. Will not judge me
2. He will think about and plan his future
3. Respects me
4. Has a kind heart
5. Enjoys talking and discussing topics with me
6. Knows how to listen
7. Will say he is sorry when necessary
8. Motivated
9. Plenty of energy
10. Looks after himself physically
11. Good manners
12. Not aggressive
13. Considerate
14. Well-groomed
15. Loves good food and wine.

These are 15 items out of 40 I had on my own list and believe it or not I found all of them in my dream man. Well, actually, apart from one – 'likes to cook'. I'm sure my husband won't mind me revealing that. He tells me that he likes to dine at Café Robyn every night. A fun thing to do if you have the time, or you can plan ahead, is to make your eating area into a little restaurant that you give a name to, just as my husband does. You can make up little menus on the weekend or for Sunday lunch. This adds such a fun element to eating together, and maybe he can be the wine waiter and the one who clears the table!

Now, back to the list. Ensure you think about the traits that you have disliked previously in someone, then write the reverse on your list as a positive. Also, really think about what you want on your list. Don't just put items like 'plenty of energy' or 'highly motivated' if these things don't really bother you at all. Some of you may think you have to write down all the perfect qualities there are in a person – but if they are not really important don't list them. Maybe you don't care if he is a generous person. Remember, only write down what is truly important to you in a relationship.

CHAPTER 3

Making changes to yourself

Now that you have a list of requirements in a partner and have taken a good look at yourself to decide if you need to make any changes to your life or attitudes and beliefs, you actually have to do something! Yes, you do!

When I met my dream man, a friend said to me that it was a good thing that the man I had just met was different to the usual type that I go for. Simple as that. I just needed to wake up to myself and see that I was making bad choices over and over again. Once you know your errors in choosing, you know what not to look for in a mate, or if the problem is within yourself, you know to start working on yourself each day.

ATTITUDES

Have friends/ex-partners told you that you are bossy, jealous or selfish? If you have sincerely looked into yourself and discovered that there may be merit in what they have told you, then it's time to turn over a new leaf and show people that you aren't that way. Of course, this won't happen overnight, but you can just practice a little each day. Try creating your own little daily mantra, such as 'people tell me I am a very giving person', or 'people tell me I am a good listener and never bossy'. Make up your own to suit the changes you want in yourself. If you say it enough, it *will* happen.

These changes you have decided to make may not be about what we have just previously discussed. They may be more material, such as changing your job, apartment, or relationship with family members.

If you want to make changes within yourself, say, because you are a very jealous person or have emotional issues you are carrying around, the best people to talk to are counselors or similarly qualified professionals. If you are open about your problems they will be able to work with you to change. You may not be happy or comfortable with the first counselor you have a session with, so do try a couple until you are relaxed and know that you will be comfortable talking to them. If you have a partner and are starting counseling, make sure you tell them so that they can give you their support. Never think there is something wrong with you if you have to go to counseling. You have made a great decision to make your life better.

WORK LIFE

If you are unhappy in your work, it will be hard to have a great relationship with someone, as you will never feel completely happy with yourself. You should be satisfied with the work you are involved in. Too many of us have stayed in positions that we aren't satisfied with for all sorts of reasons. Now could be a good time for a change – if this is what you are wishing for.

FINANCE

Another common source of unhappiness are financial problems. Do you find that you never have any money in the bank because you are overspending or not being paid what you are worth? It's really important to know how to budget and live within your means until you can improve on your financial situation by getting a raise, or a new job and starting to save.

I can't stress enough how important it is to save, no matter how small the amount is. If you start saving regularly you will have a nice little nest egg before you know it. If you feel that you just can't save or don't know how to budget, go and see your bank and they will be able to help. That's what they are there for – to help you look after your money wisely.

This is why financial goals are important. Whether it is a car, house, holiday or just rainy day money, you need to plan and save. We all love shopping, so make sure you shop around for the best interest rates on your savings. Many couples part ways due to financial stresses so feeling confident about your financial situation will really make a difference to improving your relationship. A regular direct deposit into your savings account will ensure your path to financial security.

Make your bank work for you and have them review your accounts regularly to see if they can make savings for you on fees and rates. Never just accept bank fees. If you feel that the fees you are being charged are excessive, raise this with your bank. Look for comparisons with other banks. Do they charge these fees? If you don't ask the questions, you won't be satisfied. By taking charge of your finances you will be satisfied that you are doing everything to improve your financial position and reducing stress and worry for yourself. By following these tips you will have bettered yourself and financial situation and be organised to meet your dream man.

PHYSICAL CHANGES

Some women have fabulous personalities, but still struggle to meet someone worthwhile. In these cases, perhaps a style makeover or some healthy weight loss could be helpful in rebuilding confidence in your own body. There is an abundance of styling professionals that will cater to a variety of makeover requests and ideas, all you need to do is make the appointment!

If you are concerned about your weight, make an appointment with a dietician or your local doctor who can set up a healthy lifestyle plan for you.

If you feel that you look good on the outside, confidence will follow. If you are confident, the way people react to you will change.

We've all seen this on those makeover shows where the 'bag lady' goes into the boutique followed shortly after by the gorgeous well-dressed shopper. How differently they are treated! Unfortunately, we live in a society where we are judged on first impressions, and it is important to make a good first impression and be well-presented. This says something about your character. It tells people you have some discipline and pride in yourself. That's not a bad thing.

CHAPTER 4

Life after divorce

For all of those ladies that may be divorced or going through a divorce, this chapter is about what lies ahead and what you may be going through emotionally. When I first decided to proceed with my divorce, I honestly thought at the age of 41 that there couldn't possibly be anyone left out there for me. How wrong was I?

These days the world is full of divorced men and women, which is unfortunate, but the way of our world at present. I tend to think that your first marriage can be a bit of a trial run that will lead to a happy second! There are also couples that have been together with the same original partner for many years and are still madly in love with each other, so it just goes to show, it is possible to meet the man of your dreams first time around. Maybe these folks learned their lessons earlier in life than the rest of us.

The first time I realized that there may be some hope of meeting someone was when I attended an art gallery exhibition and met a charming man who asked for my phone number after chatting with me at the event. The next day he contacted me and we dated for a few months. Even though this relationship didn't turn out to be a serious one, it did make me realize that I had some worth. Feelings of self worth can easily be removed from your emotions when you are going through a divorce. It's very important to understand your worthiness at this time. If you don't feel worthwhile, it is a great idea to get some counseling just so you can get an expert's view of your world and yourself. I think the world would be a better place if we all took time out to have some counseling every so often in our lives. Whether you are going through a divorce, grieving over the death of someone close to you, sibling rivalry, other problems with relatives or the like, counseling really does help to improve your life.

It's best not to enter a relationship too soon after a divorce, as you need time to heal and plan which direction you would like your life to take. Once you are certain about what you want, then that's the best time to proceed slowly and carefully. You don't want to make the same mistakes.

Once you are content in your mind and know what you want out of the next relationship, you can move on and make positive and informed decisions. I have a wonderful friend that helped me see the light. I just started dating my husband and I said to my friend 'he's not the usual sort of guy I would go out with'. She said, 'Well, that's a good thing!' I felt like I had been hit by a lightning bolt.

CHAPTER 5

Two is better than one

It has been statistically proven that people live longer if they are in a 'living together' relationship/marriage). Take a look around at the older people you know who are not in a loving partnership and you will see lifeless, sad and lonely individuals who cannot be bothered to cook for themselves and find moving through life a struggle. Of course, it goes without saying that this may not be their choice. Even if the relationship isn't perfect, couples find enough happiness being together and sharing the daily chores, eating together, conversation and the like. It makes sense, doesn't it? Of course there are the financial savings and attributes as well being in a live-in relationship or marriage. It can be a burden as a single person shouldering all the bills and the daily emotional problems that can present themselves.

Another aspect I always notice in older people is their grooming. Two people can ensure each other's grooming is up to standard. An older single person quite often may not pay attention to these details. This could be purely because of failing eyesight, whereas if they had a partner they would have a better chance of noticing these things. You may not be concerned at present about these things, but they are ready and waiting for all of us in the future, unfortunately. What a good feeling it is to know you have someone looking out for you and your wellbeing.

Some of the great positives of being in a partnership or marriage will include the following.

1. Laughter for two is much more enjoyable.
2. Having a trusted partner to run ideas past and discuss important issues.
3. Conversation – try having a great conversation with yourself.
4. Healthier eating patterns.
5. Keeping up contact with friends and having a social life is easier. Notice how you receive more invitations when you are a couple. A lot of women won't invite single women to events, as they feel they are a threat.
6. Help around the house (see Chapter 17, 'Living Together').
7. Having someone to take care of you when you are unwell. It's always good to have someone bring in a hot lemon drink or a bowl of hot, homemade soup to help you get through the flu!
8. Reservations for two, not one – think about it.

CHAPTER 6

Endless possibilities

Believe it or not, the world is filled with endless possibilities, but because it doesn't come and knock on our door when we would like it to, we start feeling that it is all too hard. I understand this feeling. What it really comes down to is laziness. Yes, laziness. Life never promised to give us everything we want without having to put some blood, sweat and tears into it.

Don't forget, this is a project and a long-term one if you really think about it – once you find your dream man, the work doesn't stop there. As with anything in life you have to keep working and reassessing as you go along.

If you think about your goal as a project, then you will be able to sit down and identify your goals and the means to achieving these goals. Take a look at all the options readily available to you.

Make sure you always read the weekend sport and entertainment events section. Your local council will have a website page devoted to what's on for the month and most of these are free events which attract many people from all walks of life. Think of these as endless opportunities for you to meet your dream man. You don't have to go by yourself – take a girlfriend, but never more than one. Most men will tell you it is not so bad to approach one or two women to strike up a conversation, but more than that can be a deterrent and you definitely don't want that!

Excluding free events, there are plenty of options available to you as a single woman to find a man. When you think about it we only need one likeminded person to make up a relationship with us and that person probably will be interested in doing the things that you like. So, sit down and think of all the activities that you like to do and there is a good possibility you will meet someone who also enjoys these things.

Your options include, but are not limited to:

1. Charity
2. Out and about – sporting clubs, art galleries, events, concerts
3. Classes
4. Family and friends
5. Online relationship sites

Charity

Charities are a great way to raise funds or become involved with a number of organizations. The number of people you will meet through fundraising is immense. The fact that you are in this position leaves open many possibilities to make contact with a variety of people from all walks of life.

Most charities have some sort of ball or several social occasions every year, so this is a great way to get out there and meet new people. Fundraising or voluntary work offers many opportunities to meet new people as you will be in a position to contact anyone and any business that you think may be open to helping out with a donation.

Most organizations are frequently bombarded with requests for donations, so please be humble and do not exert pressure as this is a major turnoff. If you don't succeed one year, you may like to ask if the person or company would mind if you contacted them the following year. This is polite and will still keep the door open for you. By being humble and polite, you will be able to meet a new set of people. One of them might be your dream man. Remember, this can be a numbers game and you have to meet many people to grow your circle to increase your opportunities for possible dates.

Setting up meetings to discuss possible fundraising will certainly widen your circle of acquaintances. You will not only have the opportunity to meet new friends but to put something back into the community. Organizing charity events is also a great way to meet new people.

Out and About

It's an important part of life to be fit and healthy, so take time out to think about what sports or activities you enjoy. This doesn't mean you have to be involved in a team sport. Joining a club is another ideal way to meet people.

Many clubs will have social evenings as part of the clubs activities and you may enjoy making new friends who just might be able to open some doors for you.

It's very simple to say 'Hi' or 'Morning' when you are jogging or walking around a gym. It is easy to meet new friends at a tennis club if you join the social competition days or evenings. Team sports are great as there is the need for communication. Now you may say, 'but the team players will be of the same sex'. While this is true, it means you can make friendly acquaintances who may just open up your social circle. A walking club will include members of both sexes, so here is an opportunity to make immediate contact if you desire. Once you have established some verbal contact, you have left an opening for that person to start conversation at that moment or the next time.

Make a list of all the physical and sporting activities you do or would like to participate in and think about how you can expand these activities into meeting more people. You could organize a golf day or a Pilates picnic day – anything is possible if you are willing to put some work into it.

I found that I met a number of interesting people at art gallery exhibitions. Opening nights are fun, and it's a great way to meet new people as you immediately have a topic for discussion – the art! Perhaps you can comment on a piece of art you are studying at the exhibition to someone else standing and observing. Many galleries have the option of leaving your contact details and will send an invite to the next exhibition, which may attract the same or different social set. You don't have to attend all of the exhibitions, but it is a great way to make an initial contact with someone, male or female. Don't disregard making friends with women as this could lead to introductions to potential partners and, if not, maybe just a great new friend.

Classes

Wine/art appreciation, cooking lessons, fitness classes and so on are a way to expand your social circle and perhaps meet your dream man.

Never underestimate the value of a good cooking class. These days, classes are not only attended by females but many males as well. Look at all the interest generated by cooking shows on television. Everyone from 5 to 65 seems to be watching it! If it's a hands on class, you may be placed in a group that includes some interesting males who could be worth getting to know or keeping as a contact. You know they must be interested in cooking, so surely this is a good sign? You never know what their friends may be like.

Just making friendly contact or conversation allows you to find out a little bit about this person and maybe it would be worth inviting them to your next barbecue or drinks with friends. Perhaps you could suggest you get together and try out some of the recipes you have been shown. It is great to have a few extra new faces at a summer barbecue and you should always ask them to bring a friend.

Family and friends

Often, friends and family think that they have the perfect match for you. Although they have known you for a very long time they may not understand what you are looking for in a life partner. I'm not saying disregard any blind dates, but in my experience these 'potentials' were always unsuccessful. The other thing about meeting or dating a friend's friend is that you may be put in an awkward situation if things don't work out. These are just some things to think about before you proceed down this path.

On the positive side, if you have a wide circle of friends there can be many opportunities to meet friends of friends or relatives of friends in a social setting. Many people have met their partner whilst socializing with friends and have ended up having successful relationships and even marriage. If you are open to meeting people through many different introductions then your possibilities of meeting the one for you will greatly increase.

Online dating sites

This is where I had the most luck at meeting serious people interested in a relationship, and where I met my husband. See Chapter 10 'Getting Started' – that's where I will give you all the hints and tips for searching online. In the meantime here are some statistics regarding online dating sites.

1. 11% of American adults and 38% of those who are currently single and looking for a partner have used online dating sites.

2. Online dating is most common among Americans in their mid 20's through mid 40's. Online dating is also relatively popular among the college educated as well as among urban and suburban residents.

3. 66% of online daters have gone on a date with someone they met through a dating site of app and 23% of online daters say they have met a spouse or long term relationship through these sites.

4. 53% of internet users agree with the statement that online dating allows people to find a better match for themselves because they can get to know a lot more people.

CHAPTER 7

Power of knowledge

When is the last time you took a course or studied a subject of interest for enjoyment or just to educate yourself?

One of the great joys in life is obtaining further knowledge for empowerment and growth. There will never be a shortage of subjects to study, so choose a couple of topics you are interested in and either enrol in a course or visit your library to see what is available on the subject. The more you are interested in a subject the easier it is to study. What interests you? Cooking, interior design, architecture, history, gardening, wine, languages, travel? The possibilities are endless.

The broader your interests, the more you will have to talk about with your partner, and the more he will see that you are your own woman, with your own interests. This is an important aspect of a healthy relationship as no man would want an uneducated partner, without their own opinons, who was unable to have an intelligent discussion with him or his friends.

If you really don't have time to study or do a course, just read the newspaper and make sure you are up to date with global current events. Most men love to sit down and discuss the news and share their thoughts; even if it's only the current sporting events! As much as women love to sit down to talk, analyze feelings and emotions and perhaps discuss the day's events, men don't necessarily want to do this every day and admire intelligent women who can converse on other, broader topics.

Men will offer respect more easily when they know they are dealing with someone of equal intellect. Respect brings trust, and a partner may find it easy to sit and discuss other personal topics with you if they think you will offer good advice or have an interesting opinion on a subject.

You don't have to wait to be in a relationship to start studying or learning. The sooner you start, the better. Just think how interesting and capable you will be when you finally meet your match. You may even meet him while you are doing a course. You'll have more to talk about.

It's true what they say about a way to a man's heart is through his stomach. I love to cook and have completed a few cooking courses over the years. My husband thinks I cook him something different each night, which I don't, of course, but that's what he tells everyone!

CHAPTER 8

Learn to love

I have to jump on my soapbox here and say that I have met so many women, especially divorced women, who want to have a relationship tailored around their requirements. They think 'I want this and I want that'. No mention of the man's feelings or what he wants. Remember, a relationship is a two-way street and not just about you. *You* genuinely have to love this man for himself and not what he can provide for you materially. You can't expect him to conform to *your* wants and needs. Material assets have far less benefit to your relationship and overall happiness than your emotional assets.

Show your love. After being together for a period you may become accustomed and relaxed in your partner's presence. Always show you care in the moment, reach out and hold hands while he is driving or walking with you down the road, at a dinner with friends or any other situation that you find yourselves in. You don't have to hold hands all night, but this spontaneous act will show how much you care and enjoy being with him. It's a great way of showing love, especially if you are not good with words.

The best way to get the most out of a relationship is to *give*. (See Chapter 19, 'Giving, Taking & Compromising'.)

Ask yourself, have you always been in a relationship for the right reasons? Did you genuinely care about that person? If you didn't, then you need to correct this before choosing your next partner. While you may not have been looking for material things, maybe you have been with a partner because you relied on them to make you feel good emotionally. You can never expect another person to be responsible for your emotional health. Learn to love yourself first. You've all heard this a million times before, but it is true. As women, it can take us a long time to have confidence in ourselves as we all want to solve everyone's problems and can often put ourselves last in line to receive.

If you are looking for a long-term relationship, you must learn to love the other person's mind. The body will grow old, but the mind will mature and develop when two souls are connected.

When doing some research on how to find out if you truly loved someone for the person they are, or for more selfish reasons. Here is what I came up with. Test yourself!

1. When (if) you say the words, 'I love you', do you really mean it and are you willing to do anything for that special person?

2. Do you understand how your partner feels? Do you try and control them?

3. Do you love unconditionally? Don't attach stipulations. If you are only with that person so they enhance your life, then it is not unconditional.

4. Do you expect nothing in return? Giving love does not guarantee receiving love.

5. Realize you can lose the one you love. How does this make you feel? Do you think you are lucky you have this person in your life?

6. Do you have absolute trust and don't harbor suspicions.

7. People who are truly in love don't take pleasure in their mate's disappointments and failures. Do you?

8. Do you think of things to make the other person happy?

9. Do you insist your way is the best?

10. Do you use sarcasm or ridicule your partner?

How well did you do in the test?

Make some notes next to the question or on a piece of paper. Sometimes I find writing feelings down puts things in perspective and it is easier to ponder rather than have passing thoughts and skim through the questions.

CHAPTER 9

Growing yourself through kindness

Everyone probably thinks that if they were asked, are you a kind person? They would answer yes. But what does being a kind person mean?

Well, it can mean many things in a relationship.

The first basic idea of being kind is about how you think of humanity in general. Do you have good, positive thoughts or selfish, negative thoughts? It would be honest to say that most people would have a mixture of both over time.

If you focus on only having good, positive thoughts, which won't happen overnight, you will be surprised at how your positive attitude can change to how you view the world and the world views you. We've all had lots of experiences in our life that make us who we are, and because of these experiences we may have built up barriers or coping mechanisms that aren't flattering to who we really are. If we realize that we all have some unflattering traits, then we can start to examine them and put some effort into a more positive approach.

In my experience, men look respectfully at a kind woman. Someone that shows kindness to others is held in high esteem. You will often find that because some men find it difficult to express their feelings on a daily basis, they enjoy seeing a woman who is generous to others or has positive thoughts. Remember, I am only talking about relationships here and not all the fabulous men that are involved in charity work.

I have found over the years that to be involved in charitable works allows you to be open and aware of the way other human beings live their lives and what they may have to deal with. Being aware can grow the mind before making harsh judgements about people and this has to be a good thing. Being open is the key thing here.

How often do you think about performing a kind deed? As small as 'I will cook my husband his favorite dinner tonight'? Maybe your neighbour is ill and you can take them a meal or visit for a cup of tea. Just spending time with people that need this is a great therapeutic benefit. How about doing something bigger, like taking a reading class for the kids at a school or helping out with a charity event? Time constraints will limit each person to what they can give, but it's a good feeling when you know you have helped someone.

Being kind also extends to being kind when you have differences of opinion with your partner. Never let yourself become derogatory or personal about someone when you are having a difference of opinion. Be fair and remember that your partner has just as equal right to their opinion as you do.

CHAPTER 10

Getting started: online research

For all the ladies who feel that online dating is not a suitable method for them to find a relationship or maybe are a little frightened, please reconsider. In the first instance I totally rejected participating in online dating after one of my friends suggested I try it. I thought these sites would be riddled with serial killers and stalkers! I think I would be justified in saying that this is definitely not true, but you do have to use your common sense just as you would under any other circumstances.

It took me two weeks of serious daily searching to make contact with my dream man and we are still deliriously happy today. That sounds smug I know, but it can happen for you too!

During these two weeks I made contact with five or six men that I had researched and felt may be suitable. After a couple of phone conversations with these men, I found that they weren't as suitable as I had thought. There wasn't anything wrong with them; in fact, they were interesting, intelligent people and would make great partners for someone – but they were not who I was looking for. I eventually narrowed the field down to two men, who I went out on dates with.

The first one was a disaster, with me having to listen to everything he loved talking about – himself. The second meeting was with my future husband, how lucky was I?

My advice to you is that you make the contact with the potential date. This is your project, so you have to do the research work.

When you go online, there are parameters for searching and I think I entered that I wanted to search for candidates of my choice within a 20km (12 mile) radius. Most sites allow you to take a sneak preview at their database, so I would recommend taking a close look at the type of people that are on there.

You may want to join several databases. After all, this is a numbers' game. There is a wide variety of men on all databases, but there are a few popular sites that you may feel more comfortable using due to their reputation or privacy policies.

Most sites require you to complete your personal details and the specific likes/dislikes/age group that you are searching for. The more specific you are, the better your chances of really meeting someone you are looking for. I can't stress this enough – be honest and specific. A photo of yourself is optional, and I would highly recommend keeping your photograph protected by a password and not showing it until you feel it is appropriate and you have developed a rapport with a potential date. Many women may not want it to be known they are searching perhaps due to past relationships, friends or employment factors, so this is perfect to have the photo protected. Meeting your dream man should not be based around how someone looks. It is best for you to check out the personal details and find out if they have the qualities that you are searching for. If you eventually see a photo that is so far apart from how that person described himself to you, then you can move on and nothing has been lost apart from time. When you know about a person's personality, lifestyle, likes and dislikes, it can lead you to view that person differently rather than just meeting someone who is like a blank canvas that you know nothing about. It can make a big difference in your judgement.

When you join a website you will be asked to create a user name, so don't worry about your real name being shown on the site. It is important you *do not* place a photograph on the site that does not reflect your true age and current physical shape. By conjuring up a false image, you will only cause disappointment and mistrust if the person you are meeting thinks they have been talking to a 'younger model'. You are in the middle of a life project and you don't want to ruin your chances by telling white lies. This is your future you are dealing with. Nobody wants to be deceived from the outset.

Go forward as you mean to finish. If you really feel that you want to look younger, go and talk to a doctor about physical enhancement but never lie about your age or weight! If you feel you have to lie about your weight, this is telling you something and you probably need to think about doing some exercise or showing restraint in what you are eating. Some people I know of have not posted true-life pictures of themselves and instead used images that were more flattering than they look presently. Remember that you are looking for someone that will love you for your true self and not an image from the past. Hopefully, you will love yourself too and should be body confident and know what a great person you are. It's tempting of course, but you aren't showing your true self. Just think of the happy surprise your contact will get when he thinks you look better in person than how you described yourself or looked in the photo. Go ahead and have a little confidence in yourself. As the girl in the advertisement says, 'You're worth it'.

When writing your profile, have a list ready of all the specific traits you would require in your future partner. As I've said before, the more specific you are, the better your chances will be. I wrote on my profile which political party I voted for as this was important to me. I seriously could not have been with anyone that didn't think the same way politically. Politics is an issue that can be a touchy subject for many people.

This is your opportunity to ask for everything you ever wanted – physically, emotionally and financially in a partner. You may not get everything but you may come very close to what you want.

Apart from noting the personal attributes you desire, and likes and dislikes, make sure you are specific about how you like someone to dress, fitness, hobbies and so on. If you are not into unkempt, flabby men you need to be very specific by mentioning what you are looking for. This will rule out a lot of time wasting. If physical attributes aren't important, then don't mention it. Remember, this is all about what *you* want – not the male model that magazines portray as our ultimate 'love gods'.

Never disclose any of your financial details at any stage in the online dating process. There are plenty of predators out there just waiting for the right financially secure woman to come along and support them. Unfortunately, this is common today and I have learned the hard way myself. I have also come across many similar stories to my own about these financial predators and you must be on the lookout. I always try and look at my past experiences as though they were my learning curve to get to where I am today with my loving partner.

It is important that you keep focused, even if you have had contact or dates with several men that may not have been suitable upon meeting. This is a numbers game – so keep going and don't get disheartened if you don't find your man straight away. Your dream man is out there and you are going through the necessary motions to get to him.

Be specific about how far you would like someone to live from you. You don't want either of you having to drive hours to see each other. Over time, this will become a drain on the relationship. It's often very difficult to make long-distance relationships work. If you have a love of animals or a strong dislike for them, make it clear in the beginning. It may save you a lot of time and energy.

If you only want to enter a relationship with a view to marriage, definitely include that as well – some candidates may not be interested in such a serious commitment. This will weed out all the men you don't want to waste time with.

Remember that while the man you meet may not be right for you, he is likely someone else's dream man. If you keep this in mind, you will be less tempted to think you are not making progress when in fact you are. The more dates you go on, the more you will find yourself becoming very aware of what you do and don't want. Maybe you will add a few items to your list of wants and dislikes but with this project 'practise makes perfect'.

You may want to alter your profile online to be more specific if you are noticing the right type of person is not contacting you. Don't wait to be contacted, you should be searching, emailing and approaching any potential dates that you think may be suitable. Devote yourself to this each day for an hour or so. Remember that this is your project, you must go out and get what you want – don't wait because it isn't coming to knock on your door.

Above all, it is most important to just be yourself. Never try and be someone else or your façade will be removed in time and will cause disappointment or dismay. Your dream man is someone whose love you want for who *you* are, not for who you have pretended to be.

CHAPTER 11

Meeting someone by chance

I would love to say that meeting someone while you are out and about is the most natural way to meet your life partner, but you must realize what you see is not what you get upon first meeting. You won't know anything about this person or his character until you've spent a considerable amount of time getting to know each other. If you have time on your side, by all means go for it. Face-to-face meetings are great for those who are not in a hurry to settle down, and are quite happy on the dating scene. Alternatively, if you don't want to spend a significant amount of time having to pry out information from a person to find out what they are all about, then you should look more closely at online dating sites.

Many guys find it difficult to go up to a woman and start a conversation, let alone ask her out on a date. This could be due to shyness or rejection in the past. Your dream man could be one of these people, but sitting in his comfort zone.

Always be aware of your male surroundings and don't be shy, feel free to make eye contact and smile if you see someone that you think looks interesting. The smile will let him know that it is fine to come over and start a conversation with you.

If you are still interested in going out meeting people in the course of your day-to-day life, there are many opportunities for you, so please make sure you take them. Always talk to people about themselves and not about yourself. Most people love to talk about themselves and will think you are a terrific person just for being interested in them. If you are a shy person, this is a great way to take the spotlight off yourself. I used this method many times when I was much younger and it really works!

Of course this method works well with online dating as well, but at least in that scenario, you will have some vital information prior to your meeting. In all situations you have to be very aware of who you are talking to, just in case you come across people that are deceptive. Hopefully you are insightful enough to weed these people out prior to any meeting.

If you are young, meetings by chance or opportunity should not be a problem, if you are older it is certainly more difficult to meet people if you are not frequenting bars, sports clubs, nightclubs and other venues like this. Women who have a responsibility at home with a child may be unable to wait for the right occasion to meet someone by chance. It really depends on your circumstances, so you have to make the call on how you think it best to meet someone.

CHAPTER 12

What do men truly want?

This chapter is devoted to the male voice on the subject of relationships and what men feel is necessary for a successful partnership. Relationship books and articles in women's magazines and newspapers, often tell us that men on the dating scene are unsure of how we want them to act around us. Are they supposed to be macho? Are they supposed to go along with the equality deal and leave car doors unopened, allow us to pay for half of the bill, do the inviting out for a date? I've been reading for a long time now that men are feeling confused.

Another subject worth addressing is the way modern women treat a man. I think there has been so much pressure on women to become superwoman, having the career, babies and husband all beautifully managed that many of us have become so independent that we may come across as being somewhat aloof.

Even though we all know how capable we can be in this day and age, there is no harm in allowing a man to show us his instinctive protective side or his strength to open our jars or change the light bulb. Of course, we can all do this ourselves, but I really believe men want to show off their male skills to us. It doesn't hurt to pretend to be a little bit delicate sometimes, in fact it can go a long way. I've heard some men talk about losing their male identity as the women they meet don't seem to need them for much at all in the relationship and they feel left out in their role. These are all serious comments, and I think we need to take stock of how we treat our men. If you think you are up for superwoman of the year, why don't you try taking the back seat for a while and allow your man to take control.

Men are quite simple beings really and mostly want the same things that we do – read on.

Here is a list of the top 10 things that men want from their relationships. You'll be surprised to see how many of these items would be on our list as well.

1. Be sexy in the bedroom
2. Keep the romance alive
3. Always tell the truth
4. Sometimes men just like to go into their cave so silence is appreciated
5. A good home cooked meal to share
6. Companionship

7. Laugh at his jokes, no matter how many times you've heard them
8. Listen when your mate needs to talk or unload about a problem
9. Marriage
10. Men do not like game playing so delete this if you are thinking of trying it.

An interesting and insightful book to read on the subject of men is *Men are from Mars, Women are from Venus* by relationship counselor John Gray.

The best insight this book gave me was how to deal when men go into their 'caves' when they're stressed. Gray says that women tend to discuss their problems with friends, whereas men like the time out to be able to distance themselves so their brains can focus on something else and then go back to the problem when their minds are refreshed.

I agree wholeheartedly with this as I see it not only in my own relationship but in many others. After reading Gray's book, when my husband wanted space, I dealt with it in a completely different way. Previously, I don't think I understood that he wanted some time alone and thought he didn't want to be around me. If I just respect his wish for a little space he will come out of his 'cave' when the time is right. However long it takes I don't mind, as I know he respects me for allowing him time out to think strategically about any worries or stresses he may have.

CHAPTER 13

Making the right moves

Now you have made initial contact with potential dates that you find interesting and have been communicating electronically and maybe through some phone conversations, now is the time to make your moves.

Once that you have made contact with a potential date, it's time to really get to know the person. A face-to-face meeting should take place on neutral ground, like a café, so neither party feels pressured to stay longer than needed.

It really all depends on how many phone conversations you've had and emails you have written before your in-person meeting. I would suggest at least a couple of phone chats so that you can get a sense of the person you are about to meet. You may want to have coffee or a drink after work. If you are having a drink and all is going well, limit yourself to one or two drinks as you want to make sober decisions and remember everything this person is telling you, especially if you want to make notes after the meeting. Meeting in a public place for just a refreshment leaves you the option to terminate the meeting if this person is not who he portrayed himself to be. My husband and I had several phone conversations and many emails before we met in person and ended up having a five-hour date! Time flies when you are really interested in talking to the other person and getting to know them.

If you are going to see someone that you have not met through the Internet and have previously spoken to, I would suggest you meet for a short period of time first off to ensure that you still feel the same way about this person. If you don't, upon second meeting, it is quite easy to leave after a coffee or brief conversation.

The worst thing that you can possibly do on the first date is to talk about your previous bad marriage or dating experiences. This person will not want to hear about it and if he starts going down this path with you, it is not a good sign. Although I say it is not a good sign, I wouldn't stop this conversation as it's important to find out what this person is really like. Let him be himself and you will find out quickly how he thinks.

Does he ask questions about you and your job, family, interests, your goals in life? If a man is actually interested in you for yourself he will want to find out about you, not just tell you all about himself and his achievements. How boring and selfish! It's not easy on the first date, but if there is some interest and spark you will know it.

It probably won't be love at first sight, and I would warn against rushing into anything, but if there is some interest from both sides then you should definitely pursue this with another meeting.

If you find that you are immediately physically attracted to this person, take a small step back and take a look at the person's qualities. It is important that your judgement is not clouded by their physical attributes. Of course the physical is a bonus, but you don't want to focus on the physical in the beginning. Sometimes it takes several dates to really get the spark going from a physical aspect, so it is important that you focus on the other person's other qualities from the outset.

Your mission is to find out everything you need to know about this person (that matters to you), in the least amount of time. As much as you need to enjoy your date's company and have a good time, your aim is to find out if you are suited and if this person has the qualities and attitudes you are searching for in your dream man. This is not difficult as you will find most people love talking about themselves if asked a question. Don't be afraid to ask questions. This is essential *but* please do not come across as though you are interviewing him – this is not a good start.

You should appear and I say 'appear' to be relaxed and confident. Be light-hearted and work your questions into the conversation so it doesn't appear to be a fact-finding mission. Always add a little humor in where you can. If you are wanting to find out what type of relationship your date is looking for you must ask, especially if you want marriage as a possibility. Most men are not going to come straight out and say they are looking to get married, but they will refer to a serious monogamous relationship if that is what they want.

If you think all the right signs are apparent, then there is no need to continue with the basic questions as you have begun on good terms. Your questions may stir undesirable answers. You still do need to find out if this person has extreme views on anything that may affect the way you want to be treated. For instance, your date may think women should do all the housework or are not equal to men in the workplace. The earlier you find out if this person has any undesirable aspects to his personality, the better. These are usually self-evident, but some undesirable traits may be deeper.

Most people feel easy talking about themselves and feel relaxed in doing so; this brings out their real feelings and opinions.

Don't forget that men are looking for their perfect mate as well and will want to size up your qualities and nature as well. Make sure you show your best personality traits and always have good manners. Hopefully this comes naturally, but you may like to consult with a good friend for tips if you don't feel confident.

If you are going out for a lunch and the guy pays, take this as a sign of good old-fashioned manners, which for me are a very basic requirement. Good manners and etiquette are things that are on the decline these days. I'm a bit of a traditionalist, but I wouldn't have it any other way. I believe that a woman should be feminine and a man should be allowed to take the lead in social situations. It really doesn't matter how far we have come in modernity with equal pay for equal work, which I wholeheartedly support, I still believe that the basics of a male and female in a social situation will always work best if we just play out what comes naturally to our gender – femininity and masculinity.

If you think the lunch or coffee date is not going according to how you planned, whatever you do, don't leave early. End the meeting on a light, pleasant note, remembering that you don't have to make any commitment to continue contact. Just thank the person for their time and say you will be in touch. I would advise a short email or text to say thank you for the meeting but you don't think there is any future there for the two of you. Leaving earlier than expected can be rude and hurtful. If you are just having a coffee or a drink, you may like to say at the end of your date that you have another appointment and thank them for their time and company. Everyone's self-esteem is left intact this way; it's no fun for anyone to be blatantly rejected. You must never be disrespectful to prospective dates as you could run the risk of offending him, and, in any event, we don't want to ruin the female reputation. Men are just as sensitive as we are, so always keep this in mind if you need to let someone down, do so gently.

Your conversation during your first date should be about getting to know each other and shouldn't shift into sexual preferences, political or religious beliefs at this early stage. If you know that you both share the same religion or have the same political view, then it's okay to bring it up. Talking about sex early on is a big warning sign. Someone that is truly interested in getting to know you would not even contemplate making lewd or sexual comments. Remember this is a project and keep your ears open for any warning signs, as well as indicators of the personality traits you are looking for.

Once your date is over you may like to review your list and see how many items you could tick. You're not going to be able to check off a lot after only one date, but it will be nice to know if there are a few things you asked for on your list.

Although this plan sounds more clinical than romantic, if you want your dream man – stick to it. It does get easier and it is the beginning that's the hardest – just like laying a foundation for a dream house.

Apart from your list, just think about how you feel towards this person after your first date. Do you feel good about being with him? Does he make you feel comfortable or uncomfortable? Would you like to see him again and if the answer is yes, then ask yourself why? The answer to these questions will reveal why you like this person and for what reasons.

Hopefully, if it went well and all the right signs are there you will have another date. I would wait to be invited by this person at this stage for the next outing. You can still send an email or text saying thank you for a lovely time spent together, which will indicate that you are interested in seeing him again. I think this is necessary as your date may not be that sure if you are interested or not. This email or text will be a sure way of letting him know your feelings. As an alternative, you may like to call them, but I always think it best to keep it to a short email or text just in case the feelings aren't mutual, and to avoid any long pauses and silences on the phone, which can be very awkward. If your meeting wasn't successful, just move on to your next candidate or look forward to your next date if it was a success.

CHAPTER 14

Security alert

A good general rule for dating is to arrange for the first meeting to take place in a public place.

Do not leave your meeting point with your date in his vehicle to accompany him to another destination. This is a getting-to-know-you period, and it will take a number of regular dates before you are sure that his character is good. Obviously nobody can predict this 100 per cent of the time, but you must take care and be aware as you do in everyday life. This goes for any new people in your dating life, whether having met online or through a club, friend, class, networking, or other avenue.

Never go to his home in the early stages. If he is having a barbecue or similar with family and friends, it should be fine, but don't put yourself in a situation where you are alone with him. In these early stages, always leave the address where you are going with a friend and details of the person you are meeting. You may want to ask if you can bring a girlfriend to this sort of gathering as it is great moral support when you are in a completely new situation with people you have not met. On the positive side, it is a good sign if he wants to introduce you to family and friends early on and maybe include your friends and family to meet his. This will give you the opportunity to see how he interacts with his family and friends and how they interact with him.

Don't share your address details until you are quite sure this person can be trusted. It's very easy to have trust in someone you have been emailing or talking to on the phone, but you never know what the person is like in reality. Don't be afraid by all of this, but you do need to be aware. It's probably exactly what your mother told you when you were younger. These rules apply whether you are dating via the Internet or meeting by chance or introduction.

Never leave your handbag alone if it contains personal identification details. You can make yourself vulnerable to having your personal belongings and details checked. Your mobile phone is a link to help, so never leave it where it may be stolen. This is common sense, of course, but you shouldn't be too relaxed about your safety in the early stages of dating.

CHAPTER 15

Signs along the way

Many of us at times in our lives have accepted bad behavior from our partners that is clearly unacceptable. This usually goes back to low self-esteem. I really urge you to take steps to correct this immediately by seeking professional help, through counseling.

Once you have overcome your low self-esteem or lack of confidence through counseling and reflection, you will feel as though you have woken up from a deep sleep – very refreshed and viewing life in a much clearer light – you will understand what is acceptable and what is unacceptable behavior.

Here is a checklist of unsuitable traits in a partner for you to consider.

Does your current partner tick these boxes:
1. Irresponsible?
2. Never shows up on the time?
3. Unreliable?
4. Swear frequently around you?
5. Puts you down verbally in front of friends?
6. Is he physically violent?
7. He gets fired rather than promoted on a regular basis?

If you can tick any of these boxes next to these items it's time to change your life *now!*

Life is too short to tolerate anything but acceptable behavior, and please tell yourself you deserve this basic right – because you do. If you don't take steps to rid yourself of the negative situations in your life, you won't be able to move on and become a happier person who is living in a happy and contented space. If you are not happy you cannot have a happy relationship. It's so easy to start the process. As Nike says 'Just do it'. No excuses, just sit down and make a plan that suits you and carry it through.

The first stage is the hardest, but you will wonder why you didn't start your plan earlier once you are on your way.

You get your life back – priceless! If you really don't think you have the strength to leave all by yourself, you must enlist help from reliable friends, family or community advisers. There are probably plenty of people that you know who will be only too willing to help you as they are probably already aware that you are living in unacceptable circumstances. Friends and family always seem to see this before we do, so listen to them.

Aside from the checklist of bad signs, there are several other signs that appear in the early days of dating that should set off red flags in your mind.

1.   He says he has somewhere he must be regularly but doesn't tell you who he is seeing or what he is doing.
2.   Asks for money from you.
3.   Dates you during the week and not the weekend.
4.   No obvious job history.
5.   You catch him out telling you lies.
6.   You don't trust him 100 per cent.
7.   He's not really interested in your opinion, only his own.

If you think you see any of the signs listed above, it's probably not a healthy decision to continue your relationship, so remove yourself straightaway. Nobody has to put up with this behavior, so tell him to *be gone!*

CHAPTER 16

What comes next?

You've been on a few dates now and you have decided that you really like this person. If you feel it's reciprocal, then it is a good idea to find out if you both would like to make your relationship exclusive.

Talking about serious topics like this is not always comfortable, but you should feel confident nonetheless as you are looking after your future. What's the worst that can happen? He might say no to exclusivity. There, you would have your answer. You would know that he is not what you are looking for. It is important that you find out the status of your relationship as early as possible, and if you are looking for a long-term relationship then make it known that you are looking for this end result. You will need some positive feedback from your potential dream man to ensure that you should be continuing. There is no point in going on if he doesn't want a long-term commitment. This is something that must be discussed otherwise, you will waste a lot of precious time. If you can't communicate at this stage openly and honestly you will no doubt have problems down the track.

If you both decide this is what you want, then you can proceed getting to know each other more intimately and seriously.

Once you have decided together that you want to proceed with a serious relationship, then you can really start to find out about each other's likes, dislikes and little idiosyncrasies. Just experiencing some of each other's hobbies or interests will give you a good insight into the type of person they are and the life they live. Can you see yourself with this person long-term? In the early days of our relationship I would cook a meal at my home and take it over for my now husband and his daughter to share. By cooking for your man, this shows that you care. Making a meal takes effort, but is very enjoyable when made with love.

At some stage you will have to ask yourselves about living together. When? I always think it takes two years of serious dating to get to know a person well enough to be able to make a decision about living together. Living together should not be rushed into as it is a serious commitment for both parties and a huge upheaval.

When my husband and I discussed moving in together, we had already talked about living together, and that if it worked out, it would be a natural progression to marriage. Keep this in mind when you are moving in together.

Living together is a great test of your ability to compromise. Compromise usually means settling a dispute by mutual concession but I use this word as an action taken prior to a dispute. I use it as meaning being caring enough about the other person's wants and needs to be mindful and not want your own way all the time.

As it turned out, he proposed to me much earlier than I expected and it came as a great surprise. We were fortunate with our living together but I guess we were considerate and able to compromise wherever necessary. As I've said before, being able to compromise is a big key to keeping the two of you together.

Always make sure you have something to go back to just in case it doesn't work out. Don't sell everything you own, such as your furniture, your apartment or house, to move in with your new partner. In terms of furniture, if you can, put it into storage, you can pay for storage on a monthly basis, which will give you a backup plan until the two of you want to make a permanent long-term commitment where you share finances and property and you are comfortable letting go of your old stuff.

If you are a property owner, and not living in your home, it is a good idea to rent it out while you're not there. Always make sure at the start that you have separate bank accounts. This is purely a safety precaution for your future and a very important one.

There are many things to consider when you want to live together, such as whether you both will live at your place, his place or a new place? If you decide to move in with your partner, it is important to discuss where your belongings will be going and if there'll be room for your treasured personal items. The worst thing you can do is move into someone else's space and lose your own identity. You must be able to keep this and make a footprint in the new living space of who you are.

CHAPTER 17

Living together

Now you have made the move to live together, the work really begins. You will discover little habits that you may not have noticed prior to moving in together. This is just your settling-in period, so give it some time to get used to living with another person. Don't start being negative or complaining about his ways until you have worked out how to deal with them in a positive manner.

There is a saying out there about the two certainties in life being taxes and death. Well, I would like to add another one to this list. Housework! It never seems to go away.

How often do we hear children and men say, 'she's such a nag'? We probably called our own mothers nags when we were teenagers. Aren't we lucky to be out of that stage of our lives? Hang on a minute, have we become our mothers? Really?

Yes, maybe. Take a look at your dialogue with your partner and see if he calls you a 'nag' or if you find yourself having to constantly ask for help with household. If this is the case, you may be sounding like a nag!

Don't be worried, it's curable. The frustration that you are experiencing must be dealt with appropriately, not by going on and on about helping out around the house, or finishing the odd-job that needs doing. It's easy to start ranting when we feel that we really shouldn't have to ask more than once – but our priorities may not be the same as our partners.

Everyone deals with life's chores in different ways and just because you don't get the response you want immediately, you can't expect them to change to your ways when you want. Here, I will show you how to improve your technique when asking your partner to complete chores, without nagging.

There are two groups of men out there is this world. One group is openly agreeable to household chores and the other is *not*.

For the latter, you can address which chores they will do by agreeing to the chores that you/he will do prior to moving in together. Whenever your partner has completed his work, always praise him and tell him what a great job he did – but don't be patronising! If he always knows he will be rewarded after he's done some chores he should be happy to do these tasks. Some extra rewards maybe required depending on the man. Men love to be told how appreciated they are. Often we don't praise them as much as we should. Women are the ones that are usually complimented on the way they look, or a recipe they have made and so on. How often do you hear this with men? Something to think about ...

Apart from household chores, there are always other outdoor or maintenance jobs that have to be done, usually by a man. One potential solution for getting your partner to do these jobs is to offer a reward that had an expiration date on it such as, 'if you clean out the garage I will give you the TV for an entire Sunday or make breakfast in bed for you on the weekend'. It's tit-for-tat, and really it comes down to sharing all the chores so you can spend more quality time together.

If you are really upset about something your partner is doing – like turning up late for dinners that you have cooked or not phoning when he said he would – just wait until you are both relaxed and calmly tell him how this makes you feel. If you say that this behavior upsets you and ask him to help you out by fixing this, it is much better than accusing him and being demeaning. Everyone responds to a pleasant ask for help rather than nagging or using an abusive tone.

Women tend to lash out at men due to their own bad experiences and don't want to be hurt again – so they go on the attack or become suspicious or 'act out' in many other ways. You mustn't let your previous life experiences dominate what is happening in your life today. If you do, there is a good chance that you will lose your partner.

At his work, my husband adds humor in his meetings with his staff so he is not seen as a 'nag'. Most humans respond well to humor and don't feel as though they are being pummelled into subservience every minute of the day if you inject a light-hearted but meaningful piece of humor. Try it and see for yourself.

Wouldn't it be a nice surprise for your partner to see you have taken the garbage out or emptied the dishwasher if this is one of his designated chores? Conversely, he may make the bed or put on a load of washing for you. Just everyday tasks, but these little acts of kindness and consideration really help to cement a relationship, especially if one of you is under a bit of stress or running late for work or an appointment.

One of the things that I like to do for my husband is to search for recipes that I can make and he will enjoy. He always lets me know how much this is appreciated.

Always remember to say 'thank you' and how much you appreciate any act of kindness. You and your partner won't think twice about doing those extra chores if you both know how much they are appreciated.

CHAPTER 18

Medical clearance

It takes time to get to know one another and feel comfortable in each other's presence. I would recommend that you don't sleep with your new partner until you have established that you both would like to pursue a relationship and you feel that there is the start of trust between the two of you.

How long this takes is up to the two of you, but you will know when the time is right. A couple of months of dating is a good period of time to have worked out whether or not want to sleep with a new partner.

Don't cloud your vision with lust! This is vitally important to you moving on with your relationship, so please take this seriously.

You can explore that once you have established a firm mental connection. Everything in a relationship has a right time and place, so don't rush it or you will be sorely disappointed. Don't worry if he puts pressure on you – you can just explain that you want everything to be perfect and getting to know him is the most important thing for you at this stage.

I didn't allow my husband to hold my hand until after we had several dates and I knew that we would move further down the track into a relationship. The whole reason for this is that when you hold someone's hand you are basically sending signals that you are very keen and want to be with them. Be very sure before you do this. It will take time. My husband told me that he thought I wasn't interested when I wouldn't hold his hand, but I explained at the time how I felt about it. He was mature enough to understand and actually respected me for it.

Once you have reached the appropriate time and have decided to become sexually intimate with your partner you should take some time to discuss each other's medical and sexual health.

While this can be awkward, if you want to remain clear of any sexual diseases, you and your partner must have an AIDS and STI test before you take your relationship further. We don't hear too much about AIDS or HIV these days, but it's out there and it only takes one person to transmit it to many others. Read *The Wisdom of Whores* by Elizabeth Pisani and you'll see the sexual disease statistics and sexual practices of some people are astounding.

Some men will be averse to this, but it is your life that you are taking control of. You will also have to discuss any other parts of sexual history that is relevant to your current relationship. Now is the time for honest communication. An AIDS and STI test is easy and can save you much heartache in the future.

Remember there is only one of you and you need to take care of your physical and mental health.

If your partner is against taking this test he may be hiding something, and you should either delve further or question the relationship. Both of you should have the respect for each other you deserve. Nowadays you can't be too careful. Any decent person will have a full understanding of why you are doing this and will respect you for thinking about the wellbeing of both of you. Having the test will also show his commitment to your relationship.

CHAPTER 19

Giving, taking & compromising

How often do you argue with your partner about weekend plans or which movie you want to see? Keep in mind that it's not the end of the world if you don't get to do something in particular on a specific day that you wanted to do. Both of you should just enjoy being with each other, no matter what you are doing.

If your partner has asked you to join him at an activity and you are not the least bit interested – join him anyway! He's saying he wants to be with you and loves having your company. You don't have to enjoy the outing itself, but you may be surprised what happens if you show some interest in what your partner enjoys. You may even find you develop an interest and will want to go next time he asks. Don't be closed off to everything. Have an open mind. If your partner is aware that a motor show is not exactly your thing, but you still go along with him, I'm sure he will be happy to repay you by going to a cooking class or even, dare I say it, a 'chick flick'!

As my husband is so busy with work, I cherish the time we have together so much that I'm happy doing just about anything with him. One of the things I wasn't particularly keen on participating in was fishing, however after only a one-day experience I was 'hooked'. We both love to fish now and have had many great experiences fishing together with friends when we can. One of the things that my husband did for me was attend a cooking class with a well-known chef. He now loves to participate in these classes and always asks me when we will attend another.

So you see, it's all about just being together and not focusing on activities that you think will satisfy only you. It's so easy to close yourself off to different experiences, but broaden your horizons and open yourself to new opportunities. You'll be amazed at how fulfilled both of you feel.

Some women flatly refuse to try different hobbies or holidays that may be out of their comfort zone. This can really stifle a relationship. If he wants to go on a fishing holiday and you want to go on a chefs tour of Italy, then maybe agree to do one holiday per year. Compromise, and you can do both! Maybe you can do both activities in one year if you are lucky. Think of all the memories and things you'll have to talk about when you've been on trips that both you and your partner enjoy. I've enjoyed a lot of fun and laughter participating in adventures that I have thought I would not enjoy but ended up having a ball. Life is too short to live in a box.

Generally speaking men are more adventurous than

women, and it's good to be taken out of your 'safety' zone every now and again. This doesn't mean you should give in to everything your partner wants to do, only that you shouldn't be selfish and just do what *you* want to do. Be flexible – he'll love you for it. It's the best feeling being loved and appreciated. You'll soon agree that this, giving and taking, is much better than just taking in the relationship. There's never that good feeling at the end when it's just all about you and what you want.

Although this may sound one-sided and as though I'm promoting 'giving into the male'. In truth, I am assuming your dream man is giving back as much as you are giving. If he's not, then he probably isn't your dream man. He will start to respond in kind once you have started the ball rolling. It's good to be first. Don't wait for the other person to start changing or giving.

You'll be amazed at how your actions will ignite changes in your relationship for the better. You should be receiving as much attention as you are giving or at least receiving whatever makes you happy and content. This should not be a one-sided relationship where you are doing all the giving. One thing to remember is that this man is not solely responsible for making you happy. You must be reasonably happy and comfortable within yourself to start with, so don't think the point of meeting a man is to just fulfil you and your own happiness.

You may not experience a lot of happiness while constantly giving in your relationship. A happy balance of giving and taking needs to be struck. Just take a look around at your friends' relationships and see if you can find signs of unrest because one partner is taking more than the other. Some men or women are happy to put up with this because they are too lazy to execute change or they are scared of being alone. There's no need to worry about that. A whole new world of relationship happiness is out there just waiting to happen. There are only two types of people in this world – male and female, regardless of sexuality – so it can't be for lack of choice even if you have to test out several before the right one appears for you.

While I certainly believe in equal pay for equal work, when it comes to relationships we have to go back to the basics of what satisfies a man and what makes a woman happy, so that the relationship is ultimately successful.

Two of the words that have come in my own journey are 'compromise' and 'communication'. These two words seem to say so much about the basics or ground rules for a satisfying relationship. You must have these two ingredients to be successful.

CHAPTER 20

Frequent flyer points

We all love to be rewarded, and paid compliments, it's important for our psyche. Ask yourself – do you give compliments and thanks to your partner or only receive them? If you don't, it's time to take stock and start giving some out. Often, men like to be complimented as well and as often as we like to be complimented. Try it and see the response you get. It will be a positive one.

Make sure you always take a 'girl's look' at your partner before going out on a date and say something nice about their appearance or even their cologne, but note that if your compliment is not genuinely warranted, you may have to address a fashion or etiquette issue. Some men don't have a clue when it comes to buying clothes or personal grooming. Maybe you can introduce the art of a manicure to your man. I often file my husband's nails on the weekends and he loves and appreciates it. This is what he needs you for. You are probably more equipped to help out here and he will really appreciate your time spent offering ideas and shopping mornings. This is a great skill and will give you extra mileage points.

My husband and I love going shopping together for him. He loves having his own 'stylist' and really appreciates that I take the time to show him what looks good on him. These days he rarely shops without me as he respects my judgement when it comes to buying new suits or shirts. I know that I earn many points for helping him look put together in the clothing department.

CHAPTER 21

Changes in your relationship

Circumstances, whether emotional, family or financial, will dictate reviews and reassessments, a need for flexibility and adaptation with your partner and possibly your lifestyle. Don't expect your situation now to be exactly the same in 20 years' time.

You may indeed be more in love after 20 years, but maybe your financial situation or your health has deteriorated. Perhaps you have increased your wealth substantially, but if life throws you some curve balls and circumstances change, you will have to adapt and learn to cope with the differences these new circumstances make in your life.

There may be times in your life where your cash situation may not be as good as you would like. It is good to put away a little extra cash for you and your partner for these times. If you both would like to get ahead and pay off that mortgage or a loan you will need to plan on how you are going to achieve this. How much of a difference would some extra cash make in your life? Well, it could make a big difference and I'm not just talking financially either. Think about how this money was made. Perhaps it meant extra long hours and traveling away from home for extended periods, which has led to reduced relationship and family time. Sacrifices will have to be made in order to achieve your goals of financial advancement. Flexibility and especially tolerance from both partners is important. Understanding and communicating will be the key.

One of the biggest changes that can occur in a relationship is taking the other person for granted. If you can identify this early enough, it's easy to correct. It essentially comes back to always being able to communicate effectively. It's important to ask for your partner's opinions even if you don't actually need a second opinion. The important thing is that you are including him. Obviously, you don't need to bother your dream man all the time with his opinion on fashion, for example, but take the time to ask what he thinks of this event or the new project you are working on. It will help keep you in synergy with each other.

How do you talk to your partner? Do you still speak to him in the loving way you used to at the beginning of your relationship? Do you make him feel valued? Do you brush his opinions off or talk down to him? It's very easy to become so comfortable with a person that we forget that they are the most important individual in our lives and the most loved. We start treating them as though they were an unwanted telemarketing caller. Listen to yourself the next time you speak to your partner. Just be very aware and correct yourself if you find your tone is demanding or nagging – this is one of the biggest complaints received from men.

If someone gave you a quiz about the last two months of your relationship and asked you what your partner was thinking and feeling, would you be able to answer. Would you know if he has any new projects or goals that he would like to achieve? Have you taken the time to discuss these things with each other?

This is why you shouldn't take one another for granted. It's all about sharing and being genuinely interested in what your partner wants out of his life as well as what you want out of yours.

There are so many changes that can occur in a relationship and we need to be aware and prepared for them, whether they are financial, emotional or physical. If we plan and communicate for these changes we'll be prepared for anything that comes our way.

CHAPTER 22

Sex!

Why do I find so many women complaining about their partners or husbands wanting sex? What's the big deal? If your partner is the man you hope to spend the rest of your life with, then give it up, ladies.

Men, generally speaking, have greater physical needs than we do and let's be honest – how long does it take? The mere fact that your partner wants you, tells you he's not going anywhere else and, believe me, there are plenty of women out there who will jump at the chance to be with your dream man. You have to treat your dream man with tender loving care and ensure all his needs are met. Stop complaining. If he's looking after you outside of the bedroom, then the least you can do is take care of him inside the bedroom.

Your partner in life should be your number one priority.

Hopefully, you are enjoying sex with your partner and if not, why not? Are you too tired or stressed? It's up to you to do something about it. Change your job if you have to work too many hours and are no longer enjoying it. Do you feel overloaded at home with chores?

Writer Joan Sauers says: 'A lot of women would like a lot more sex if only their partners could do things a little differently, both between the sheets and around the house. Familiarizing our partners with how to excite us sexually and introducing them to the proper method for changing the vacuum cleaner bag will eventually lead to greater happiness for both sexes.'

If you are feeling stressed, mutually satisfying sex will take it away temporarily and relieve any of the tension that may have been building up during the day or week. Try it when you are feeling under pressure and not really in the mood. You may want to try it again after this experiment, as it really works! You'll both be happy and content as a result of taking the time to enjoy each other and relax.

Are you at that stage in your relationship where your sex life is becoming predictable? Easily fixed. Why don't you suggest trying new positions or even locations? Do you always have sex at bedtime? Change the time. Surprise him with a gentle nudge in the morning, even if it means setting the alarm clock a little earlier now and again. How about a surprise in the middle of the night? A new baby doll nightie? A romantic dinner date? How about candles and champagne with a bubble bath for two, or a back rub. It's really up to you to decide what is going to work for the both of you.

CHAPTER 23

Reservations for two

'The way to a man's heart is through his stomach.' Have you ever heard the women in your life say this? Well, it's true. Old-fashioned, you may say, but it's a great way to please your partner. He will really appreciate your efforts.

My husband always tells people that I've never cooked him the same meal twice. Of course this isn't true, but it's a great compliment to me and lets me know how much he appreciates the time I take to cook something nice for him – this serves to encourage me to cook for him all the time!

We always go out once a week to a restaurant, which he tells me is his appreciation for the wonderful meals I've cooked during the week. One idea, is to make a deal whereby you volunteer to be chef if he takes you out somewhere nice to dine on a weekend for date night. Date night (see Chapter 27, 'Date Night') is the evening when you both have time to go over the week and spend quality time with each other.

You must never lose sight of each other's lives and how each person is feeling. This is your opportunity to dress up and be admired by your husband all night long. He'll definitely appreciate your efforts. If you are with your ideal man, then I'm sure he will make an effort for you too.

Always compliment him on how he looks. Your partner's ego needs a boost too, you know.

This being your one special night together without interruption should be a quality evening of conversation and talking about topics you enjoy. Perhaps make a couple of mental notes on what you could say to your partner that would make him amused or surprised.

If you have a great relationship your conversation should flow freely and you will not have to worry about what you will converse about. Just don't make the conversation all about you and your problems. Make sure you listen attentively if he wants to unload about his work problems, though, as this is his opportunity to let you know what is going on in his life at work and it is important for him.

It can be interesting to share or try each other's meals. You will both have had the same dining experience if you know what each other tasted. Remember, it is a reservation for two!

CHAPTER 24

The kids!

Have you been in relationships where your partner already has a child or children? How much stress do you think this added to your relationship? Would you enter a relationship again where there were children involved?

If you are still in a happy relationship with a partner's offspring, then congratulations. You have succeeded in being an unselfish and considerate person. This area of being in a relationship with someone else's children is vast and accepting and living happily with another's children really can test a relationship, but if you can work it out then you can probably look forward to a happy future together. The key is consideration and communication. Much of this will depend on the age of the children. Younger children tend to be more accepting, whereas teenagers can be volatile and unaccepting to start with. If you have patience and can let time work through to a solution whereby the kids accept you, then go for it.

If you are not willing to put in the hard yards, then I would not recommend this for you. Resentment could build over the time you want with your partner and would probably eventually end the relationship. This can work vice versa of course if you are the one with the children.

Your age is also a key factor in a relationship where children are present. If you are still relatively young and don't have any experience with children, this whole arena may seem foreign. If, on the other hand, you have been in a similar situation with children and are understanding of their needs, then you will be better prepared. Maturity is very important when dealing with children, and your partner will want somebody strong and accepting of his responsibilities for his family. You won't win any points by demanding more time.

If you are in a relationship with children present you still have to make time and maintain your relationship with your partner. Always make time for date night and weekends away when possible. This will keep the spark in your relationship and not make it feel so humdrum. It is easy for a man to leave the child minding and child raising to the woman if he isn't reminded of his responsibilities to your relationship as well as to the children.

Often men complain about their partner putting them to the side while they attend to the growing children. This is seriously wrong. How can a relationship flourish if the two of you are not in it together as equals? Remember that your husband was there first, before the children came along. Your children will grow and leave home. What is left – a husband or partner that you no longer have fun with or share anything in common? Your job as parents is to love and raise your children and guide them through life as best you can, without taking away from your relationship with your partner. You must take time out to spend together so you can be a couple and not just co-parents.

CHAPTER 25

Love vouchers & appreciation

Once you have your dream partner, the secret to keeping him is to keep the relationship alive and well. One of the most romantic ways to keep your partner interested is to leave little love notes under his pillow or under the windscreen of his car so he will see them when he gets in his car to drive to work. When you are writing these love notes, it actually makes you sit down and think of all the things you really like and respect about your partner. If you are having trouble thinking of something to write, he may not be your dream man!

A real winner is to create love vouchers for your man. You can give him a voucher for anything, from a special home-cooked romantic dinner for two, champagne picnic or just a romantic pamper evening. I always like to pop a few vouchers in with birthday and Christmas presents. If your partner travels frequently, a great way to keep up the contact is to give him dated envelopes with vouchers for each day he is away with instructions not to open until the date stated on the envelope.

When my husband and I were in the early stages of our relationship he had to go away for nine days to the US, which seemed like an eternity. I made up vouchers for each day, and I can't tell you how much this meant to him and how it kept the relationship alive during his absence. Each day he would open the dated envelope and look forward to his voucher, while I couldn't wait to hear from him and find out how much he loved the new vouchers.

You can make your own love vouchers or print then off from an Internet site. Just type in 'love voucher' and you will be able to find something suitable in a very short time. It's best to print them out in color and use silver and gold marker pens to write on them.

Once you set the standard with your love notes, I'd be amazed if you didn't see the benefits or, in fact, reciprocal behavior. Maybe not reciprocal love notes, but something special just for you. Everyone loves to be appreciated and it's so important as human beings, in close relationships, to show your appreciation regularly rather than release negative thoughts into your home space.

Happiness is contagious, and has great rewards and flow-on effect when we selflessly give to another. Try it and see what happens. Do one small, selfless act today or tomorrow for your partner and see how much happiness you get back. You will wonder why you never thought of this before. This is all part of learning to give. If you give, you will receive ten-fold the enjoyment. One of the reasons you may not have thought of this before is because life is so busy now. That's why it is even more important to take a few minutes to think about and assess our lives, implementing ways to improve and sustain our relationships.

'Having my dream man is so much effort and trouble?' you say. Of course, it takes effort and if you are not prepared to put in the time you won't be as successful as the couples that do. That said, if you really enjoy making your man happy you will be destined for a truly long and lasting relationship. It's your choice!

CHAPTER 26

The workplace

Would you say that you have always been a supportive partner? This chapter is all about being a great support system for your partner. We all need to work and in any relationship there will be times when hard decisions have to be made in order to advance our careers. If our partner has an opportunity to advance his career in another state or even another country we need to think about the long term benefits of making these changes. Think about some past ideas your mate had or job opportunities that may have required you to move interstate, for example.

It is your job to support your partner in his career, especially if he is going to be the main breadwinner in the family. I'm not suggesting for a moment that your career or job is unimportant and of course you need to be taken into consideration, but I am referring to the situation where your partner is the main salary earner and on the upward spiral in his chosen career. If you aren't a keen supporter, your husband's career may suffer and consequently your relationship. Don't forget that when you may decide to have children, your partner's earnings will be of utmost importance for however long you decide to be away from the workforce.

It will be your job to give him positive emotional support when change comes his way in the workplace. These changes may not suit you, but if it means furthering your partner's career then you should put aside your selfish concerns and support him 100 per cent. Moving interstate is not the end of the world as so many wives seem to think. I do understand how many of you have infrastructures all in place when raising small children, but there are always alternatives if you and your partner sit down to discuss a plan to remedy your causes for concern. Think of it as an adventure and not as a load to bear. There is an old saying, 'Happy wife is a happy life' (for a husband). Well, the same is true in reverse. Start working together as a team. Being happy together is work, but only as difficult as you make it. By the way, you should want to make *each* other happy.

Always be a good listener. Take the time to listen attentively when he wants to share a problem in the workplace or discuss an idea.

Women should support their husbands or partners by making themselves available for business functions. You may think some of these corporate occasions are boring, but it will show a lot of support to your husband if you happily accept these invitations.

If you are a stay at home mum, greeting your husband or partner when he arrives home with a smile, fresh lipstick and a dab of perfume is a sure way to ensure he will be eager to come home to you. Nothing is more of a deterrent to a man than coming home to a nagging, complaining, untidy woman. There are plenty of other smartly dressed single women who will step into your place if you let your appearance go. Do you think your partner would rather look at a woman who is dressed looking fresh and appealing or someone in baggy old jeans and t-shirt without makeup and unkempt hair?

Yes, I know it is work, but that is just how it is.

CHAPTER 27

Date night

This is the precious time you and your partner can devote yourselves to talking, dreaming, planning or just holding hands with undivided attention. When you are at home, there are always distractions – the phone ringing, emails, working at home, TV, cooking – that take your full attention away from your partner. You both need to develop your relationship and keep it alive by taking the time to find out what's going on in each other's mind such as new ideas or thoughts for the future, talking about current affairs, investment and savings strategies, holiday planning.

We don't all have the time each day to sit down and have long discussions about what we are thinking or to plan, so this time out is essential. It will bring you closer together and give you more of an understanding of where each person wants to head or if they are concerned or worried about something.

If there are children in the equation, it is crucial that you have a date night once a week. Your whole life can't revolve around the children, and when you take time to think about it, there are adults involved in your life as well as children. Neglecting the adults in the family will have just as detrimental effect as neglecting the children.

You owe it to yourselves so you can keep up a healthy and communicative relationship. If you love each other, you will both want to spend some quality time together.

Pre-plan your date nights and mark them in your diary so there is no double booking. Make a list of what you both enjoy doing socially and work your way through the list. One week it might be bowling, the next week could be at your favorite local restaurant. The main aim here is to be able to spend time together, talk and have fun. Whatever you enjoy, make sure you are able to participate together. This will always remind you of why you are with this person.

Always make an effort in your grooming on date night. You want your partner to see that you are looking your best – not the mum that has stained track pants and hair pulled back every day of the week.

Sometimes life is mundane and difficult, but that doesn't mean you can't have fun. You don't have to spend a lot of money every time you go out. Picnics, bowling, movies and a quiet drink after, a walk and a coffee are perfectly fine. These are just examples of how you can spend quality time together that's conducive to your adult communication.

It's a great time to talk about hopes and dreams, what you would like to be working towards for the future. If you don't have plans or dreams for the future, you have no future.

CHAPTER 28

In the mood!

How many of us suffer from mood swings at that time of the month or maybe you are just a moody person? I hear men all over the world groaning and pleading for the mood swings to stop. Sounds like a simple request, doesn't it? We all know, though, that moods are not easy to control and many men lack understanding about them.

The good news is that there are many ways we can help ourselves when suffering from mood swings.

Exercise is key in overcoming shifts in your mood, so put your walking or gym gear on and get to it. Even 15 or 20 minutes out in the fresh air can change your mood for the better. Just doing some exercise will give you time to mull over whatever is bothering you or give you time to sort out why you are feeling grumpy and how to deal with it in a calm and relaxed manner.

Natural remedies such as eating walnuts, almonds and pure soy products, which are high in tryptophan, contribute to the mood-boosting hormone serotonin. Try eating a handful a day if you know your moods are likely to change.

Evening primrose oil tablets also work for some women. You will have to try this for yourselves and see what happens. As with all natural remedies, you should be on the remedy for at least six weeks before you will see a difference. Just talk to your pharmacist or doctor who will know what's best for you.

If you are a naturally moody person, you may want to seriously consider doing something to control your mood swings, as nobody should have to put up with moodiness. Talk to your doctor about going down the vitamin and natural way first, before taking anything further. If you don't have a chemical or hormonal imbalance, then it is up to you to control your mood swings.

Imagine coming home to someone each day and not knowing what kind of mood they are going to be in. It will certainly put your partner on tenterhooks when he is around you and he will not be able to relax. Take the time to work out little ways of stopping yourself from snapping if you know you are about to have a mood swing. It probably won't work every time, but at least you are thinking about how to handle the swings.

CHAPTER 29

You make me feel like a brand new man!

I've mentioned previously the importance of complimenting your man when the time is right. It is so important to make your partner feel like he is the greatest man he can be.

Self-esteem for a man is an essential part of his core being. Of course, it is for a woman as well, but if we lack some self-esteem it may not necessarily spill over into our love and sex life, whereas a mans self-esteem is what drives him through life. A small compliment can make me feel better instantly. I think this is not so easy for a man as they usually like to feel they have done or achieved something to feel good.

If a man has low self-esteem, he may find it difficult to perform in the bedroom. Constantly nagging or belittling your partner could lead to his loss of interest in the bedroom. Never belittle your partner's masculinity and this includes ridicule of physical attributes such as weight or baldness, for instance. Most men will go into their caves when they are feeling low. Always be aware of this. Sometimes they just want a little time out to think and other times it may be due to low self-esteem because of something you have said. It is very easy to reduce someone's sense of self-worth, but it can take a lot longer to rebuild. Try and think about what you say before you say it; remember, once it is out, you can never take it back.

A man loves to feel needed and we, as women, love to feel we can rely on or look up to someone. You may be able to remove the lid on the jar or change the light bulb, but just look at his face after you tell him how strong he is or how clever he is doing repairs in the house. Men want to be admired and we should ensure we give our admiration whenever required. Always tell your man how much you need him and love all the things that he does for you and he will beam and puff out his chest. See Chapter 25, 'Love Vouchers & Appreciation' for more on this topic.

Never ask for material things that your husband or partner cannot provide for you. Be sure not to constantly criticise your partner for not buying you this or that, harping on about what you want. You will not only make your partner feel inadequate and attack his self-esteem, but he will feel unappreciated and unloved as you don't seem to love him for what he is providing for you. You are giving off signals that he is not good enough. He will soon tire of this and may turn his interest elsewhere, so be warned.

Be with your partner for his qualities not because he can buy your happiness.

Be a good listener. If your partner starts telling you about problems at work, or the compliments or achievements he's received in the workplace, give him your undivided attention so that he knows you care about what he has achieved or is encountering. If he thinks you are not interested or listening he may find someone else that is interested. If you feel like you have solutions to problems of his, avoid saying 'you should do this', always ask him what he thinks about your suggestion. He may or may not take it on board. At least he will know you are listening. If you have a good listener, it is a great way to unburden yourself and you'll probably work out what to do without the other person finding a solution. It always helps to have two people talk it out, though.

Even if he tells the same old jokes a hundred times and you are tired of hearing them, still listen and laugh as if it is the first time you have heard them. He will know that you have heard his stories many times before and will appreciate your consideration.

CHAPTER 30

Respect for each other

Respect for each other is such an important ingredient in your relationship. Without this, failure is sure to arrive on your doorstep at any time.

It really doesn't matter how differently you and your partner view the world, there is no excuse for not respecting your partner's point of view, wishes, desires, likes, dislikes.

If you can't respect your partner's difference of opinion and be polite about it, you have to learn to do so.

Never put your partner down because they don't agree with you, or say something that you think is silly or not to your way of thinking. Before you say anything, think how you would feel if someone were to criticise you because of your opinion.

Once you respect your partner, it really is a great feeling of comfort. I think once you respect a person, trust comes hand in hand.

Respect for a person also means not hurting them with offhand comments about personal traits or annoying habits, which we all have, by the way. You have to learn to be subtle in your comments to ensure the person will not be embarrassed or made to feel bad. For example, don't say things like 'oh, that's disgusting' if he was clipping his toenails in the bedroom. Make a point of saying something like, 'That's not very attractive to me when you do that in the bedroom, honey. Why don't you try the bathroom? You men need your grooming privacy, too, you know.'

DIFFERENCES OF OPINION

Managing your differences takes two people to initially agree on how you will handle them. If you have spoken about how you will handle your differences and disagreements, at least you know you will both be trying to manage the problem from an intelligent and not emotional and irrational stand. That's the theory anyway.

If you have a disagreement, don't start yelling or getting personal with your partner. Stick to the facts and communicate in a manner that is polite and gives the other person a chance to put their view across. Don't raise your voice; this can lead to a downward spiral and can be difficult to adjust back to a normal tone.

If you just can't come to an agreement verbally, take a breather and, for instance, each make a list of the 'fors' and 'againsts', or positive feelings and negative feelings. If none of these strategies work, and you are having a huge screaming argument, yell 'I love you'. It will be a shock to hear this and can be humorous at the time or make you see how silly your argument is and that you both should calm down.

If you find your man knows which buttons to push with you, just keep calm and remember it's better to lose the argument and keep harmony in the relationship. You'll be a bigger and better person for realizing this. I'm not saying back down every time – just pick your arguments wisely. Maybe you are arguing over something small like attending a dinner at a friend's house that he doesn't particularly care for or a destination for a holiday. You could remind him of things you have done for him in the past that you have not always been happy to do but have done so because of your love for him. This will be a good reminder and will hopefully make him appreciate your thoughtfulness. You may even win him over with the argument.

Arguments are never good for a relationship because the damage *can* last forever. Each time you have a big argument, a tiny piece of love is being eaten away even if you have made up at a later stage.

Never go to bed unhappy or mad with your partner. If you are unhappy with each other, then you must work it out before you turn off the lights. Your bed should be the place where you have your most intimate moments not fighting words or silences. If you are happy in bed, you will be happy out of bed with your partner.

Always remember, when you are feeling mad or angry your feelings are directed at the most important person in your life, so you shouldn't start to attack. Give yourself some time to think over the problem as it may not be as bad as it seemed, in half an hour or an hour, if you have mulled it over thoughtfully.

CHAPTER 32

Childlike anger

I recently read a book by Helen Andelin titled *Fascinating Womanhood*. This book was written in 1965 and has sold millions of copies all over the world. Although Helen Andelin wrote for her time, I have to agree with most of what she has written and we can still use her rules today for a successful marriage/partnership.

One of the chapters in the book was about using childlike anger when you were unhappy about something your partner had done. I really loved this chapter and want to share with you what she said. A friend of mine who recommended the book to me has used this practice and assures me that it works. I have used this method as well and it worked for me too.

Basically, what she says is that if you feel you have been treated unfairly, have been insulted or have had your feelings hurt, consider using childlike anger instead of retorting with your temper or becoming moody. Helen describes the example of the cute little girl who stamps her feet or says she will never speak to you again out of sheer frustration after maybe being teased or emotionally hurt. The way to express the childlike anger is to express it with the innocence of a child and without the sarcasm or ugly emotions we tend to give out when we have been hurt.

Learning the mannerisms of a child such as stomping your feet, turning and walking away, then pause and look back over your shoulder, even beating on your partners chest in an overacted way. This could actually bring a little humor to the situation. The use of learning adjectives like you 'big, tough brute', 'hairy beast' and 'stubborn'. Always ensure your adjectives are complimentary and will not belittle your partner. You want to get your point across that you are angry without making the situation worse. Make exaggerated threats like 'I'll never speak to you again' or 'I won't do anything for you anymore'. While at first this advice may seem very old-fashioned and naive and we couldn't possibly deal with a situation in this manner in this day and age. Believe me you can and it does work. You may have to think about what you are planning to say or act out, but it's worth the time and trouble. A little overacting never hurt anyone.

CHAPTER 33

Forgiveness

One of the things you will have to learn to do in any relationship is to forgive. Perhaps it will be forgiving something small or something more serious, but we all need to learn how to forgive. Nobody is perfect, not even you!

If you can't forgive and move on, then your relationship will suffer because at the back of your mind you will always harbor resentments and misgivings about your partner. These will surely surface when you have a future disagreement.

So, how do you forgive? You learn to weigh up how important the misgiving is compared to living the rest of your life with your partner. We all make mistakes during the course of our lives and usually the worst punishment comes from ourselves as we have to live with our mistakes. As long as we learn from them we have been taught a worthwhile lesson. Our partners will make mistakes and we must learn to forgive. Don't put that person down and tell them 'I told you so'. They are already probably beating themselves up about it mentally. Give support, and talk about the mistake and how you can correct it. Do this without raised voices. Your understanding will go a long way in helping to correct the mistake. There aren't too many things in life that can't be corrected with effort and time.

If you are dealing with a small mistake, such as your partner shrinking your new jeans in the clothes dryer – he can buy you a new pair or you can just say 'thank you for putting the clothes in the dryer, but would you mind asking me first about anything that is doubtful for the dryer'. This may be difficult to say at the time, but you can't imagine the relief they will feel. Believe me, they won't do it again.

There may be times when the mistake is more serious, for example, a financial matter or an indiscretion with someone else. These can be worked out if you want them to. It's not worth giving up your relationship for something that can be resolved. It has to be made obvious to you that your partner wants to rectify the damage done. You may both have to go to counseling to sort the problem out and to move forward, but it will be worth it in the end. Forgiveness is something that comes with time, depending on how big the 'forgive' has to be.

The 'forgive' for the clothes dryer incident is more or less instant, whereas financial or personal indiscretions will take longer. You must be prepared to make the effort to work through this and understand the other person is probably feeling the same strain as yourself. Just work on it together.

CHAPTER 34

Dressing for success

Just because you have met your dream man and he may have committed to you doesn't mean you can let your guard down in the appearance arena. You should always take pride in your appearance, not only for yourself, but also to keep your partner's eyes focused on you.

The dos and don'ts of dressing to keep your man interested:

1. Always remember when your partner tells you how good you look in something. You can wear these outfits when you especially want to please him, and know that he is admiring you. If you stop taking care of your appearance he will notice and may even pass a comment – if he is brave enough.

2. If you are wearing an outfit that is tailored and businesslike, add a silk scarf, brooch or a lacy or sheer blouse to add that touch of femininity. Soft, silky, lacy fabrics will always enhance your femininity to a man.

3. Ensure your clothes are fitted well for your body type and not overly baggy.

4. Always wear perfume and find out which ones he likes best. If he knows the names of the perfumes you wear that he likes, maybe he will buy them for you!

5. Always dress up to the occasion and not down. If you arrive at a party/function a little overdressed, it is far better than to arrive underdressed as you will feel uncomfortable all evening if you are not 'decked out' properly for the occasion.

6. If you aren't the type of person who likes wearing makeup, go as far as lip gloss and mascara with a light touch of perfume. These are the minimum required to send out your feminine vibes.

7. Ensure your lingerie is pretty as well as practical. I know we all have the Bridget Jones spandex underwear somewhere in our collections, but make sure you have a pretty collection that he will get to see. Men love lingerie and do not want to see old, faded, boring underwear. I know we all criticise our bodies in our underwear, but men just don't seem to see all of our concerns. They just love the overall picture and the pretty lingerie. Ask your man, and he will tell you, if he hasn't told you before.

8. Wear clothes that suit your body type, and not just because it is in fashion. If you are unsure of what works best for you, take time out to learn and book in

with a stylist or get some helpful advice from one of the available experts at the department stores.

9. Don't go overboard with hair styling products – nothing is more of a turnoff to men than feeling like they are running their fingers through a sticky mass of hair products.

10. Never go overboard with revealing clothes. You will lose any elegance you have tried to put into your outfit. Showing some cleavage is fine, but there is a line between tasteful and tawdry which you should be mindful of.

11. Make sure your perfume doesn't enter the room before you do. We all know what I'm talking about here. You know the woman who enters the room and fills it with her overpowering perfume? We all love perfume but it should never be overpowering.

12. Does my bum look big in this? Never ask a man this. If you think your behind looks too big to wear an item, then don't wear it!

13. Always make sure your clothes are neatly pressed. Nothing is worse for your appearance than crumpled clothing. If you aren't keen on ironing, there are many brands today that manufacture jersey silks and stretch fabrics that don't require ironing, so this is the key for you. A word of warning: Make sure you have the correct undergarments on as these fabrics can be

unflattering if we have unsightly lumps and bumps.
Best to wear the spandex on these days, girls!

14. Always make sure you have regular haircuts/color so
your hairstyle stays in shape and you have limited
regrowth. In between appointments, use at home color
products. You'll save in the long run as it will take
less time to manage. The biggest turnoff to a man or
woman is to be with someone that doesn't respect their
body 100 per cent by taking daily care of its needs.

One of the things that a man loves about a woman is her
delicate perfume or that freshly shampooed hair perfume.

Ensure your hair is always clean and healthy. Freshly
washed hair smells great and can be very attractive to a man.

A light spray of your favorite perfume always leaves a
lasting impression.

Clean, pressed clothes show that the person cares about
the way they present. No matter what your budget, this is
always available to you.

If you are going to be intimate always ensure you are
fresh as you can be. Some people's natural body odour may
not be as pleasant or delicate as others, so be very aware or
you may turn your partner off. There is no excuse in this day
and age to not be as fresh as a daisy.

Bad breath is always a turnoff and may be caused by
such things as drinking too much coffee, an upset stomach,
bad teeth or poor dental hygiene. Dental hygiene is not only

important when coming into contact with someone else, but essential for your own good health as well. Gum disease can readily occur and have a serious effect on other parts of your body as well. If you have any concerns, talk to your dentist.

Nails should be manicured at all times and chipped polish is a no-no. This includes your feet. You can tell a lot about a person by looking at their hands and feet and how well cared for they are. If you don't have time for repairs to your fingernails, sculpted nails can last up to three weeks. Alternatively, keep your nails short and clean if there is no time to spend on polishes or nail appointments.

Whatever your preferred method of excess hair removal – do so – otherwise it can be unsightly and untidy. Smooth, bronzed legs look fabulous in heels in summer and most men will admit to enjoying the feel of a smooth leg. Just as we may not enjoy a bristly man's face, many men don't enjoy the bristles on a leg or on any other part of your body. Smooth is sensual, bristly is not!

Nothing looks more appealing than toned, moisturised skin. If your skin is looking a little dull, dry or beginning to show signs of ageing, mix up some grapeseed oil or jojoba oil with your favorite body cream. Nivea cream mixes well with oils. Baby oil can be used instead, and is just as good, but the grapeseed oil has toning properties and the jojoba has a moisturising effect.

We all love the healthy tanned look, but it is important not to place your body in the sun unprotected.

The fake tan is the deal these days, *but* nothing looks worse than a bad spray tan or blotchy self-applied tan cream. Always ensure you have an even tan and don't forget to touch up the little areas that wear away quicker than most, like the feet and hands. Do your research and stay away from 'oompa loompa' look. There is no need to look overdone these days, as there are some terrific natural tanning products on our market.

CHAPTER 35

Good advice

What follows is advice and heart-warming stories from couples that have been successfully married for over 25 years.

This couple has been married for 35 years, and this is what the wife has to say about her marriage:

'We have been married for 35 years and it's always been romantic. For every anniversary my husband sends me roses for each year of our marriage. So now I get 35, and on Valentine's Day it's 37, celebrating the time we have been together.'

'I have always tried to make home a soft place to fall. My husband equates it to pulling up the drawbridge when he walks in. These lessons aren't taught and you learn as you go along. My mother would always put on lipstick at 5pm and change her apron just prior to my Dad arriving home. I have always remembered that – keeping the romance alive!'

It is wonderful to be able to pass on good advice through the generations.

'My mother loved to shop and sometimes she would only just make it home before my father. So she would get the pots out, fill them with water and they would be bubbling away when dad got home. She always said, "If the table is set and he sees the pots cooking albeit with only water (he never knew!), it keeps a man happy"'.

The following stories and advice are from women that have been married between 40 and 64 years.

'Lots of compromise. Be wise enough to walk away and only argue if it's worth fighting for. I wanted him to be happy and have a peaceful life. I was nine years younger than him and more fun. He was quite a serious person. He always said to me, "I'll wait for you to grow up – ha ha"'.

'We knew each other six weeks before we married, and the day we were married he sailed off to war. It was eight months before we saw each other again and all the letters were censored by the War Department. It took six weeks for a letter to reach home. My husband enjoyed the simple pleasures in life, and had no expectations. He was strict, often saying "we must get the house paid off", he was an upright, moral man. We respected each other's feelings.'

'My husband is adventurous, whereas I am happy to read a book. I would go along with my husband in his more adventurous activities anyway to find out if I liked them or not.'

Here is a good piece of advice that we, as modern women, should reflect on:

'Be grateful for today and all of our modern appliances that make our lives easier.'

'Don't believe in confrontation if you're not in control. You'll say something that you will regret. My husband would say, "This is what we are doing, okay, and it's my way". And I would not answer and walk away. Shortly after he would come over and put his arm around my shoulder and say, "We're friends, aren't we?" I would say, "No, we're not" for a while, but then I would come around after a time.

This advice is so true:

'To have someone love you, you have to be loveable. Who wants to come home to a nagging, unkempt wife or partner? I always looked after myself and kept trim and dressed neatly.

I still have my nails and hair done at the age of 87!'

'It's hard work every day – say you love each other every day. You can be lucky if you pick someone who has the same ethics, family morals, likes etc. You have to like them and find them generous in spirit and a kind person.'

In the end it is the mind that you speak to, not the body.

'Be friends: Expect the worst and hope for the best. Always have a positive attitude. Care more for the other person than yourself. Don't be a hysterical person. And don't try to be their mother.'

'Give and take all the time. Don't be controlling – you can't change people.'

Some people try to change the person or tell them what they want. Your partner has his own mind and can speak for himself or make up his own mind on his own. After all, he decided to be with you, didn't he? Do you think he believes that is a mistake?

Here is a very important piece of advice:

'Have shared interests. Once the children are grown, you don't want to be staring at each other wondering who this person is.

Develop interests or keep up your own throughout your marriage. At times it won't be possible, but don't let them go.'

This next piece of advice is why we have two televisions in my home!

'Always let the guy have the remote control.'

'Make sure you can do the same sex positions that you could do 20 years ago!'

'My husband thought he could keep me happy by doing the cleaning and that way he would always get sexual favors. Anytime I would come through the door and smell detergent and ammonia I would think, "Oh shit, it's tonight"'.

'Timing – it is important to get your timing right when discussing problems. Don't bombard your partner with problems as soon as he walks through the door. Give him a drink and a kiss first, or something similar to help him unwind, then you will have his attention.'

CHAPTER 36

Made with love

My husband and I both have very busy schedules and entertain a lot, so we really look forward to any time we can spend together and share a home-cooked meal. In my opinion, the old saying that a way to a man's heart is through his stomach still stands today.

My husband travels a lot and is constantly at restaurants and functions, and often all he wants is a good home-cooked meal. One of his favorites in winter is the old-fashioned recipe of sausages, mash and peas! Comfort food.

You don't have to be an amazing cook or plate up like the top chefs to impress, just make the food tasty and make dining together something you both look forward to at the end of your day. I understand this is not always practical if you have young children, but once they can feed themselves and sit at the table, you can make it great family time. Sometimes it is just not possible, but if you are in a situation where you can or there is only two of you, do make the most of it.

SEAFOOD LINGUINE WITH A TWIST

8 scallops, roe off   8 prawns, tails on
50 g (1.8 oz) smoked   1 tsp lemon rind
   salmon   1 tsp orange rind
1 tsp red chili   olive oil
1 400 g (14 oz) can   1 tsp sugar
   crushed tomatoes   125 ml (4 fl oz) white
2 cloves crushed garlic   wine
1 tbsp chives, chopped   250 g (8 oz) linguine

Sauté scallops for 3 minutes and prawns in a little olive oil in the pan. When cooked, remove to a covered plate. Add in the crushed garlic to the pan, add lemon and orange rind, chili, sugar and wine. When starting to boil, add tomatoes and reduce heat. Simmer for about 15–20 minutes until flavors are bursting out.

Cook the linguine until *al dente*. While pasta is cooking, return seafood to pan and cook until heated through. Once pasta is cooked, drain and stir through sauce.

Serve and tear smoked salmon lengths on top and sprinkle with chopped chives.

STEAMED BARRA WITH GINGER & THAI SALAD

2 barramundi fillets

10 slices sushi pink ginger
lemon wedges, to serve

SALAD

1 green mango, finely
   sliced
1 yellow bell pepper
   (capsicum)
2 red chilies
1 garlic clove, crushed
handful mint leaves

1 red bell pepper (capsicum)
2 limes, juice
1 tbsp fish sauce
1 tbsp palm sugar
1 tbsp coriander (cilantro)
   leaves

Place the fillets with sushi ginger on top of a pan of boiling water in the steamer. Turn on the steamer when the salad is almost ready. You can make the dressing the day before.

DRESSING

Combine lime juice, sugar, fish sauce, finely sliced red chilies and garlic. Shake and mix well. You may want to alter the ingredient quantities to suit your own taste.

GREEN MANGO SALAD

Slice green mango into tiny, fine matchsticks. A mandolin is good for slicing thinly, then you can chop into matchsticks. Finely slice capsicums into matchsticks. Finely chop the mint and coriander leaves. Grind the roasted peanuts. In a bowl, combine baby salad leaves, mint, coriander, ground peanuts, capsicum and green mango. Pour sauce over and leave for a few minutes to marinate. Serve with the steamed barramundi.

LAMB SHANKS WITH CANNELLINI BEANS

4 lamb shanks
800 g (28 oz) can
    crushed tomatoes
400 g (17.5 oz) can
    cannellini beans
8 baby onions

125 ml (4fl oz) red wine
500 ml (17 fl oz) veal or
    beef stock
2 garlic cloves, crushed
1 tbsp fresh thyme leaves
salt and pepper, to taste

I use a slow cooker or a heavy casserole dish in the oven for this recipe. Both methods turn out well.

Seal the lamb shanks until browned in a pan, then transfer to your cooking dish of choice. Add the remainder of ingredients apart from beans and thyme.

Add these in the last hour of cooking.

Cook for approximately 6 hours on low. When meat is cooked, season with salt and pepper to taste. You may need to slightly thicken sauce in slow cooker. Serve on a bed of rice or couscous.

STUFFED CHICKEN BREAST ROLLS

2 chicken breasts
50 g (1.8 oz) Danish fetta
   cheese
3 tbsp bunch fresh basil
5 tbsp spinach leaves,
   roughly chopped

2 tbsp coriander
1 small lime
Salt
6–8 sun-dried tomatoes
1 tbsp pinenuts

Slice the chicken breast in half, but not completely all the way through. Flatten the chicken out and make a pocket. Combine cheese, tomatoes, chopped fresh basil, pine nuts and roughly chopped spinach. On a sheet of aluminum foil, sprinkle the coriander, lime and salt. Lay the chicken breast on top. Spoon the cheese mixture into the pocket. Roll the breast into a neat oblong with the foil and secure tightly by twisting and folding ends towards centre. Place on a sheet of cling wrap and roll up, twisting ends and folding towards centre of oblong. If not secure, water will enter.

Do this with each breast. Place the breasts in a pot of water that is about 70°C (160°F). The water should be just off simmering. The breasts will cook in about 20 minutes. Remove from pot and cut wrapping away. Leave to rest for a couple of minutes before slicing into thick slices to serve.

RED PORK LOIN ON CRUNCHY NOODLE SALAD

500g (17.5 oz) pork loin
1 tbsp five spice
125 ml (4 fl oz) Hoisin sauce
½ cos lettuce
3 tbsp crunchy fried noodles
8 sun-dried tomatoes
1 red bell pepper (capsicum)

125 ml (4 fl oz) plum sauce
2 tbsp lemon juice
1 long red chili
1 packet baby spinach leaves
½ avocado
3 stalks spring onion

Marinate pork loin in five spice and hoisin overnight if possible. Cook at 160°C (320°F) for about 35 minutes. Rest for 5 minutes before slicing into approximately 10 rounds.

Make salad dressing from plum sauce, lemon juice, finely chopped chili and a little water. You may want to reduce the amount of plum sauce if this is too much for the two of you.

Combine all of the salad ingredients, apart from noodles, which will be placed on last, before the rounds of pork. Pour dressing on top.

SMOKED CHICKEN, AVOCADO & MANGO SALAD

1 smoked chicken breast
½ avocado, cut into
   chunks or slices
quality olive oil, to taste
½ cos lettuce
½ red onion, chipped
50 g (1.7 oz) goat milk
   fetta

2 tbsp caramelized
   balsamic, to taste
½ fresh mango, sliced
1 packet spinach leaves
½ red bell pepper,
   (capsicum), sliced

Mix all the salad ingredients together and then toss through pieces of the smoked chicken. Dress with caramelized balsamic and olive oil. Delicious.

Final word

I sincerely wish for all my readers every success and happiness there is to have in life with your dream partner. Don't be disheartened if it takes a while or longer than you thought. Remember you are on a journey and developing yourself as well. Keep to the guidelines and you are assured of success.

I hope to hear back from all of you with your success stories.

One last thing: I would like to put a challenge out there to a man to now write the partner to this book called *How to Meet your Dream Woman – and Keep Her!* Now that will be interesting reading for all of us!

MY LIST

NOTES ON PROGRESS